THE GREAT JOY
of
HEALING PAST LIVES

MAKING THIS
A FABULOUS LIFETIME WITH
EFT TAPPING

JUDITH RIVERA ROSSO

BALBOA.
PRESS

A DIVISION OF HAY HOUSE

Balboa Press books may be ordered through booksellers or by contacting:

Balboa Press
A Division of Hay House
1663 Liberty Drive
Bloomington, IN 47403
www.balboapress.com
1 (877) 407-4847

For such legal and ethical permission, contact the author:
E-Mail: eft-italy@libero.it
Internet Sites: www.eftitalia.com; www.cascinarosso.info

By the same author published by
Positivamente in Langa in Italy:
EFT & Vita - Book published in Italian
EFT & Life - eBook in English

Cover art provided by www.dreamstime.com.

Printed in the United States of America.

ISBN: 978-1-4525-9164-3 (sc)
ISBN: 978-1-4525-9165-0 (e)

Library of Congress Control Number: 2014902261

Balboa Press rev. date: 03/06/2014

Praise for EFT Tapping

"Put away your skepticism, this really works...I've had great results with tapping in my own life."

Wayne Dyer, PhD

"I have been using EFT for years and I find it an important tool in creating the life of my dreams."

Jack Canfield

"Have you tried tapping? I truly believe that it is a wonderful and life-changing tool."

Louise Hay

"EFT is a simple and powerful process that can deeply influence gene activity, health and behavior."

Bruce Lipton, PhD

"We use EFT in our clinic to help patients and to eliminate many forms of pain..."

Joe Mercola, DO

"I have been using EFT for years and I highly recommend it."

Joe Vitale

"EFT offers great healing benefits."

Deepak Chopra, MD

"EFT is easy, effective, and produces amazing results. I think it should be taught in elementary school."

Donna Eden

Celebration for *The Great Joy of Healing Past Lives*

A *personal word of my deep appreciation to the following reviewers who have taken the time from their demanding schedules to read* **The Great Joy of Healing Past Lives** *and offer their comments. The fact that they come from many corners of the world – The USA, England, South Africa, Iran, Germany, France, Switzerland, Italy, Australia – is a testimony to the widespread interest in healing our distant past and in the marvelous gifts of EFT.* ☺ *Judith*

♦ "In first hearing about Judith's work in healing past lives, my first response was 'It's about time someone addressed this'. I've found that while most events, circumstances, emotions or traumas can be healed fairly easily with tapping, there are times when we hit a brick wall. And while that may be a small percentage of the time, when that happens, working on past life experiences with EFT is an amazing option that almost always brings astonishing results.

As Judith describes in **The Great Joy of Healing Past Lives**, there are people who are totally open to, and believe in, past lives, while others range from somewhat skeptical to extreme 'non-believers'.

If, however, someone is willing to at least explore what may have happened prior to this life, via tapping, we are almost always astounded by the results. Judith does a great job in describing means and ways this can work with tapping. If there is another method that works better, I'm not aware of it.

Personally I've amassed a plethora of stories about clearing past life traumas and circumstances. And for my clients, that means they are able to heal, reclaim their lives and regain peace of mind. Since the risk of past life exploration is almost risk-free, it's worth taking the chance. For those who are willing, it can change their lives. Kudos to Judith for sharing her insights, wisdom and methodologies about healing past life experiences in such a beautiful and remarkable way."

Lindsay Kenny, EFT Master and Trainer
www.ProEFT.com

◆ I so appreciate that Judith Rivera Rosso has written *The Great Joy of Healing Past Lives*. Past life regression has always been an important part of my work. I have guided hundreds of regressions through the years, and there is no denying the healing power of these experiences.

What I love about Judith's approach is the way she has fully integrated the superb body-centered technique of EFT. Her descriptions of sessions remind me of something quantum -- as we tap on this body in this present moment, we can access and heal distress and pain that appear rooted in lifetimes lived centuries ago.

It is a great mystery that our current body and mind can hold these depths. Yet again and again profound healing emerges from past life exploration. I am very excited that Judith has shown us how much EFT can enhance the process.

Past life stories are deeply transformative and inspiring and they need to be told. *The Great Joy of Healing Past Lives* is a true gift to the healing arts community and to the world.

**Betty Moore-Hafter, MA, Certified Past Life Regressionist, AAMET EFT Trainer and Co-author of *The EFTFree Manual*
www.CreativeEFT.com; www.EFTfree.net**

◆ "Judith Rosso is hard to miss – and not just because she's tall. The first time I met her - at the AAMET Conference in Florence, Italy in 2012 where we were both giving speeches - I could not help but notice her beautiful way of being: sensitive, intelligent, generous, kind and inclusive. The way she moved through the room was like watching a flock of birds dancing through the skies. *The Great Joy of Healing Past Lives* is the same.

Never pushy, never assuming, always opening up to possibility and including, Judy manages to appeal to novice and expert, past-life skeptic or believer. Drawing on her extensive experience of many years and with a very warm style of writing, Judy expertly explains not only EFT, but also how to apply EFT in the fabulously rich world of past lives step-by-step – whether you or clients believe in them or not.

The Great Joy of Healing Past Lives is a practical, hands-on guide to this intricate and delicate way of using past life work to help yourself and others to experience significant shifts which, having had the privilege of exploring an unexpected past life during a session with Judy, I highly recommend.

Despite my own extensive experience with EFT, 'The Great Joy' taught me some wonderful new ways of working with clients which I look forward to teach future students. Regardless of your familiarity with EFT and whether you are a Master or a Beginner, you'll learn something from this book, for sure. It's an easy read, clearly structured and well balanced between theory and practice and, with the actual case studies adding mystery, intrigue and excitement!

Above all else, you'll learn how to open up even more to the possibility of the unseen and the not-understood, and appreciate more than ever that there's a lot more to us as a species than meets the eye.

There is gold between the covers of *The Great Joy of Healing Past Lives* and it gets an absolute and unequivocal 'yes' from me – read it!"

Bennie Naudé, Master Trainer, EFT and Matrix Reimprinting
www.deepliving.com

♦ "Simple and elegant, Rivera Rosso's method of clearing Past Life Stress with EFT tapping provides the key to a depth of healing not possible from looking at life only through the lens of our present incarnation. She points out that our current problems may have roots in patterns from past lives that need to be healed so we can live fully in our present life."

Barbara Stone, PhD, Author of *Invisible Roots: How Healing Past Life Trauma Can Liberate Your Present* **and** *Transforming Fear into Gold*
www.souldetective.net

♦ *"The Great Joy of Healing Past Lives* is a breath of fresh air. It discusses the possibility of past lives and what that might mean for us and how we can use that concept to clear the really deep stuff for our clients and ourselves.

It doesn't matter if you believe in past lives, if you think you may be connecting to someone else's life, or whether your subconscious has created a metaphor for you to connect to your deepest wounds, go there and you'll be amazed at the depth of the results.

Judith's book is a great mix of explanation, examples and teaching and I loved the quotes from all those famous people who believed they'd been here before!

Whether you work with past lives, or you'd like to and don't know how, or you don't believe that we've lived before, *The Great Joy of Healing Past Lives* will give you food for thought, new information to get the brain working and ways to experiment in working with past lives for yourself."

Jaqui Crooks, EFT Master
www.beacontraining.co.uk

♦ *"**The Great Joy of Healing Past Lives** by Judith Rivera Rosso* is an extraordinary book about the combination of two rather controversial topics: past lives and energy psychology. With great skill and patience, the author presents both concepts and how they interact with equal respect for the believer and the skeptic. Anyone with an open mind will learn some amazing tools for unlocking the mysterious world of past lives by using EFT.

Besides writing a totally clear and accessible book, the author has included many quotations from famous people throughout history who have believed in past lives. She has also included some wonderful illustrations that help make the book totally readable and fascinating. I highly recommend *The Great Joy of Healing Past Lives* for anyone interested in the possibility that past lives exist and open to learning a unique way to access that information."

Dr. Kiya Immergluck, Pro EFT Master
www.eft-tap.com

♦ "Exploring past lives is a great endeavor. It helps us avoid repeating the same old patterns, over and over again, life after life, and sorting out what we have to do, our real desires from what we've already done, our acquired memories. That's how we keep growing, and expressing our full potential.

Healing past lives is an even greater endeavor. It helps us in overcoming space, time and ego, anchoring our consciousness in the present moment of this infinite cosmic event we're taking part of and contributing to co-create. That's how we expand and enjoy the eternal journey of our soul.

This is the greatness of Judith Rivera Rosso's book, *The Great Joy of Healing Past Lives*. This groundbreaking work takes you in both journeys simultaneously, gently unfolding a new dimension of living. Through touching stories, intuition and easy techniques, it leads you across time, space and life, down the length of your invisible emotional roots, penetrating deep into the heart of your personal and collective universe.

No past is past, she states in her book, and no problem is ever confined just in one lifetime. Your past, problems and lives are all in your present, simply buried in the depths of your unconscious. Making great use of visions, imagination, and the intention to grow above limitation, she opens that door and gives you the experience of what it means to be living forever.

Intrigued by her last challenge, *'Is knowledge of past lives the missing ingredient to health and happiness?'* I now definitely need to know more about EFT. Thank you Judith Rivera Rosso for your wonderful book."

Andrea Scarsi, Msc.D., author of *The Secret of Metaphysical Science, Secrets of Meditation, Answers for the Soul,* and *Seeds of Enlightenment* www.andrea-scarsi.com

♦ "How exciting reading Judith's new book, *The Great Joy of Healing Past Lives*! I'm totally grateful to my dear EFT teacher for generously sharing with us her most intimate and revolutionary experiences."

Irmela Grazi-Knapp MD, Italy

♦ "In *The Great Joy of Healing Past Lives* Judith Rivera Rosso presents a fascinating and potentially powerful way of using Emotional Freedom Techniques. Whether or not the practitioner and/or client believe in past lives, the information here can still be of great interest and benefit."

Brad Yates, EFT Practitioner & Teacher, Personal Development Speaker and Author of *The Wizard's Wish* (EFT for Children)
www.bradyates.net

♦ "Many of my clients don't "believe" in past lives. And they don't have to. If the conscious or subconscious needs to be Joan of Arc to solve an issue, why not? Judith is very clear in the importance of honoring your clients' beliefs and their own wording and that is precisely why her using EFT with past lives works so well.

The Great Joy of Healing Past Lives is wonderfully clear teaching with terrific client examples. Read it to become a better practitioner for yourself or others, no matter what your belief system is."

Karin Davidson, EFT and Matrix Reimprinting Trainer and Practitioner, Co-author of *EFT Level 1-3 Training Resource Course Books*
www.HowToTap.com

♦ "In this book packed with fascinating case stories about her EFT work on past lives with her clients, Judith Rivera Rosso offers us some interesting approaches and techniques to clear present life-time issues through these past experiences – or more specifically, by working on moments of past lives. As she writes, 'This work is not about death – it is, instead, about life and living free from unwanted negative baggage from our past and distant past.'

EFT is a powerful holistic and truly universal healing aid; however, its action can be stopped dead (no pun intended) by our limiting beliefs. While the concept of reincarnation may seem unacceptable to some and ridiculous to others, it is a reality for many.

How do you know about your past lives? What is a past life memory? How do you know if what you are experiencing is really coming from a past life?

What you consciously know is really not all that important, as it is your subconscious mind that holds, in its great wisdom, all of your memories and past secrets for you. What is important is all that you may be feeling about an experience and how this relates to what you are experimenting in your life today. Just like energy or Spirit, emotions are ageless and timeless.

Right from the beginning, my EFT and coaching practice has lead me to work with people from all over the world, holding different beliefs. My clients have shown me over and over that we have a lot to learn and gain by keeping our minds open to different alternatives while on our amazing EFT journey.

I have worked with hundreds of people like Bill, Jim, Bob, Bertha, Marie, Eddie, Evelyn and the others who we meet in *The Great Joy of Healing Past Lives*. Some named their experience a 'past life', some were happy to think it was a 'metaphor' for their present issue.

It doesn't really matter whether you choose to label these experiences 'past life memories', 'metaphors', or even 'hallucinations'. What does matter is your willingness to go with them and into them, without any further rational labeling or questioning – just as Judy shows us to do.

Judy generously shares here with us the many details of her subtle work with her clients and the original EFT style she has developed to help them clear their past life experiences. She explains how we can safely work on these experiences to make our present life better and help our clients do the same, even if this sometimes means stretching a little bit some limiting beliefs. *The Great Joy of Healing Past Lives* is definitely a must-read for all!"

Diane von der Weid, Certified EFT Trainer & Practitioner, Certified Coach
www.eft-suisse.ch

♦ "There is so much that can be resolved with EFT, by working on issues in this lifetime that many EFT practitioners neglect to consider the importance of unresolved issues from previous lives.

However, as Judith Rivera Rosso points out in *The Great Joy of Healing Past Lives*, in order to be fully free in the now, it is of utmost importance to clear and heal any influences that past lives may have on this lifetime.

Judy provides us with excellent tools and tips for how to joyfully heal past lives which can be implemented by a novice or an expert EFT practitioner."

Andrew Lewis, International EFT Trainer
www.emofree.it; www.emofree.com.au

♦ "What a joy it is to have an author like Judy who understands this precious kind of work. Judy tells her story, as well as the stories of others she has helped, in order to assist us in healing and understanding how it feels to be free.

The Great Joy of Healing Past Lives helps you know what to do and how to do it in the simplest ways to get the process started for a healing that lasts."

Wade Lindstrom, Personal Coach, Jack Canfield Coaching

♦ In today's so-called modern world, it takes courage and conviction to go against the flow. The concept of healing past lives is often foreign to our "western" thinking but in her cutting-edge work, *The Great Joy of Healing Past Lives,* Judy makes the idea of past lives easily accessible and convincing. You will enjoy reading it. She writes as she lives, with her characteristic lightness, enthusiasm and pragmatism.

Others who, as I do, rely on creativity for their work must surely have experienced unexplained doubts or feelings that can be such terrible barriers not only to their art but also to their personal lives. My wish is that everyone experience the wondrous feeling of becoming free from past life trauma by opening this window that brings relief, lightness, and reassurance and thereby, unlimited inspiration. Every piece of the puzzle finds its place and all barriers are broken. How does it work? Can it be explained? Answers to these questions do not concern me. All I know is that addressing my past lives with EFT has unleashed unknown resources that have enabled me to truly express myself.

Bettina Thomas, Bettina Thomas Couture Hats, www.bettinathomas.com

♦   "Through EFT I have learned how to gain control over my feelings and therefore my life. It is fascinating to realize that this control can even go beyond this lifetime.

In order to live life to the fullest and to find harmony and happiness you need to get to know yourself and clear out blockages from the past, so that the energy can flow freely. In *The Great Joy of Healing Past Lives* Judy has made a major breakthrough; she teaches us that confronting painful incidences from the past can become a gentle healing procedure through EFT, no matter how far back you go."

Luise Bonte-Friedheim
Fashion Consultant, Milan and Paris

♦ "I love *The Great Joy of Healing Past Lives*; it is compassionate and friendly as well as knowledgeable and with a strong sense of reliable authority. Judy tells stories of supporting her clients on the journey of opening to underlying causes of their suffering and unease through the methods of EFT. Her artful approach leads naturally to healing traumas of this life and often traumas from past lives, clearing the barriers to a freer, happier and more fruitful current lifetime."

Mina Semyon
Yogina and Author of *The Distracted Centipede; a Yoga Experience*

♦ "I am 21 years old and reading *The Great Joy of Healing Past Lives* was such an inspiration on so many different levels. I feel that it has opened my eyes far beyond the casual conversations I have with my friends. And having had Judy use some of the techniques on me recently I truly believe it's beneficial to try out!

I recommend this book to anyone who is interested in learning about themselves. Whether you are new to EFT or not, it is a great read!"

Yasmin Mackay, University Student
Oxford, England

♦ "I may not know who I was in past lives and who I will be in the future but what I know is that EFT is powerful and has given me a tool to work with when I need an emotional or a physical healing, self-approval, self-acceptance and self-love. In my next EFT session, I look forward to learning about my past lives to be able to heal even more of my present life. With love and gratitude for writing *The Great Joy of Healing Past Lives*, thank you, Judith, for teaching me."

Shekoofeh Mackay, Nurse-Midwife

♦ "In *The Great Joy of Healing Past Lives*, my favorite quotation, attributed to Thomas Dewar, is "Minds are like parachutes, they work best when open". To read *The Great Joy of Healing Past Lives* takes an open mind. It will prepare you for a thought-provoking journey and allow you to benefit from an experience which you will never forget. *The Great Joy of Healing Past Lives* will also give you 'tools' that you can use again and again.

In my opinion, when you begin to experiment with EFT, the question you have to ask yourself is, "Am I ready to be healthy and happy?" If the answer is 'yes' and if you are willing to leave behind the *secondary benefits* of your illness or problem, *The Great Joy of Healing Past Lives* paves the way towards freedom, good health, richness, joy and peace with all human beings and the universe. So, it doesn't matter whether or not you believe in a past life, you must believe that you'll be healthy. EFT has changed my life; I was ready to live the change."

Antonella Ghibaudi, teacher and translator

◆ "Judy has very cleverly and intuitively discovered that healing past life trauma is also possible with EFT and her excellent book *The Great Joy of Healing Past Lives* tells you how. Any book which helps us understand that we all have the ability to heal ourselves and that all the answers and wisdom we need are within, gets my vote!

As a past life and life between lives regression therapist I am extremely privileged to witness the remarkable and often miraculous healing that comes from visiting and transforming past lives. Helping people to release energy that they may have carried with them over many lifetimes and is now manifesting in their current lives in the form of emotional, physical or mental problems, is a privilege and joy.

Knowing how to heal past lives with EFT is a valuable asset to this much needed healing modality. I applaud Judy and the important contribution she is making with *The Great Joy of Healing Past Lives*; it is a wonderful book, really well done and a fantastic achievement."

Bel Rogers
Regression Therapist and Trainer with the Past Life Regression Academy UK and Italy
www.positiveperceptionsltd.com
www.regressionacademy.com

"The real you, the immortal you, is the you that is present from body to body, from life to life."
~ BRIAN WEISS, MD
Through Time into Healing

"Your soul is eternal. Your spirit doesn't end; it merely transforms."
~ SANDRA ANNE TAYLOR
The Hidden Power of Your Past Lives

"Children all over the world have described memories of previous lives. More than 2,500 cases are registered in the files of the Division of Personality Studies at the University of Virginia."
~ JIM B. TUCKER, MD
Child Psychiatrist, Medical Director of the Child & Family Psychiatry Clinic, University of Virginia
Life Before Life: Children's Memories of Previous Lives

I dedicate this book to all those
who are willing to break free
from the limits of conventional thinking
and to their courage to do so.

Contents

Foreword   xxxi
Introduction   xxxvii
With Gratitude   xli
Prelude   xliii

Chapter 1 What Is EFT?   1

Chapter 2 How Can You Know If You Have Lived
           Before?   4

Chapter 3 New Terminology for Our Ancient Ways   8
           Past Life Stress (PLS)   8
           Past Life Trauma Sequence (PLTS)   11

Chapter 4 Energy   15
           Energy and Healing   17

Chapter 5 Using EFT to Heal Past Lives   20
           Past Life Session Categories   21
           Believer Clients   21
           Skeptical Clients   22
           Automatic Clients   22
           Clue-Giver Clients   23
           Child Clients   23
           Ourselves   23

Chapter 6 Measuring the Response of Energy   24

Three Methods of Locating Specific Events   26

Applied Kinesiology, also known as

Muscle-Testing   29

Dowsing with The Pendulum   31

The Bio-Tensor   32

Which is the Best Instrument to Use?   33

Chapter 7 Past Life EFT Sessions   36

Resistance to the Idea of Past Lives   37

Bill Felt He Lived Before   43

Intention in the Past Life Session   45

Preventing Negative Past Life Re-

Stimulations in Daily Life   51

Jack Canfield's 'Yellow Alerts'   52

Jim Improved His Vision   53

When You Share Past Life Experiences

with Others   58

Automatically Arriving at a Past Life Memory 65

Finding the Cause of Marie's Hearing

Problems   67

Paying Attention to Clues   70

Children and Their Past Lives   72

Eating Problems   76

Additional Sessions with Evelyn   79

Hallucinations or Memories?   80

Chapter 8 Do-It-Yourself Past Life Healing   82

Chapter 9 How To Do EFT Tapping   86

The Intensity of the Problem   87

The Setup   88

Psychological Reversal   88

Where exactly are those tapping points?   89

The Basic Tapping Points of EFT   90

The Karate Chop Point   91
The Setup Affirmation   93
The Sequence / Reminders   94
Your notes about tapping points: 95
The Crown Point (CR)   96
The Below the Nipple / Liver Points (BN)   96
The 9-Gamut Procedure   96
The 9-Gamut Tapping Spot   97
Some Advanced Tapping Points   99
The Wrist Points   100
The Back of the Neck & Spine Points   100
The Knees (K)   102
The Ankles (AN)   102

Chapter 10 The Future   **104**
Is Knowledge of Past Lives the Missing
Ingredient to Health and Happiness?   105

The Resource Section   **109**
Books about EFT   109
Books about past lives   111
More great books   112
EFT Internet sites   114
EFT Radio & Audio Sites   120
EFT Films   120

Epilogue   **123**
An Ode to Gary Craig   **124**
Remembering Peace   **125**
About the Author   **127**
Index   **129**

Foreword

Collective Consciousness
by Bernie Siegel, MD

Ibelieve in the power of storytelling to convey the gifts of life's experiences. Even when those experiences are unpleasant or painful at the time they are happening, truthful storytelling can help us look for and find the gifts of learning, understanding and personal growth.

Judith Rivera Rosso is a teacher who in another time might be sitting around an ancient campfire sharing stories about her experiences, as well as those she encountered on her life's journey. Today, through the pages of *The Great Joy of Healing Past Lives* she shares these stories, taken from her experience, about past lives and healing.

In my own work, I often tell and re-tell about my own experiences in what I like to refer to as the "Collective Consciousness". You might already be familiar with some of these happenings in my life.

For example, when I was four years old I was home in bed with one of my frequent ear infections. I took a toy telephone I was playing with and unscrewed the dial and put all the pieces in my mouth as I had seen carpenters do with nails which they then pulled out to use. The problem was that I aspirated the pieces and went into laryngospasm. I can still feel my intercostal muscles and diaphragm contracting forcefully, trying to get some air into my lungs, but nothing worked and I was unable to make any sounds to attract help. I had no sense of the time but suddenly realized I was not struggling anymore. I was now at the head of the bed watching myself dying.

I found it fascinating to be free of my body and a blessing. I never stopped to think about how I could still see and think while out of my body. When blind people have a near death experience they do wonder how they can see when they are out of their bodies. I was feeling sorry my mother, who was in the kitchen, would find me dead but I thought it over and found my new state preferable and intellectually chose death over life.

Then the boy on the bed had an agonal seizure, vomited and all the toy pieces came flying out. He began to breathe again and I was very angry as I felt sucked back into my body against my will. I can still remember yelling, "Who did that?" My thought as a four year old was that there was a God who had a schedule and I wasn't supposed to die now. So an angel apparently did a Heimlich maneuver on me is the way I would explain it today.

I really do believe there is a schedule we create unconsciously because of my later life experiences. Twice I have had my car totaled by people driving through red lights and once I fell off our roof when the top rung on my wooden ladder snapped off. In none of these incidents did any significant injury occur to my body. Someone told me it was because I had an angel and he knew his name. I asked what it was and he asked, "What did you say when the ladder broke?"

"I said, Oh Shit!"

He said, "That's his name." I will add he always shows up when I call him in an impassioned way.

My next experience was with the healer Olga Worrall. I had injured my leg training for a marathon. It was very painful and not responding to rest or therapy. At an American Holistic Medical Association conference Olga was a guest speaker. My wife told me to ask her to heal me. I was embarrassed to ask and very frankly a non-believer. Never the less my wife pushed me forward and Olga sat me down in a chair and placed her two hands on my leg. The heat from her hands was incredible. I remember putting my hands on the opposite leg to compare the heat sensation. There was no sense of warmth from my hands coming through the dungarees. When Olga was done I stood up and was completely healed. The pain was gone and I could walk normally.

Another time Olga and I spoke at the funeral of a mutual friend. After the ceremony we were standing in a deserted hallway when she asked, "Are you Jewish?"

"Why are you asking?"

"Because there are two rabbis standing next to you." She went on to tell me their names and describe their garments, which included their prayer shawls and caps. Her description of them was exactly what I saw in my meditation and imagery sessions when I had met these figures while walking on my path.

Another evening after I gave a lecture, which felt like someone else was giving it and I was simply verbalizing it for them, a woman came up to me and said, "Standing in front of you for the entire lecture was a man and I drew his picture for you." Again, exactly the face and features of my inner guide. I still have the picture hanging in our home.

My next experience came when I was telling a friend about how busy I was and she said, "Why are you living this life?" Her intention was to get me to slow down and travel less but her question sent me into a trance and I immediately saw myself with a sword in my hand killing people. My first thought was that I had become a surgeon in this life to use a knife to heal and not kill.

I spontaneously went into a trance again a few days later and saw myself living the life of a knight who killed because he feared his lord and what he would do to him if he didn't carry out his commands. I killed my wife, in this life, and her dog and was devastated by the experience. But at the same time it revealed to me why my wife's face has always had a hypnotic effect upon me and why I am so involved in rescuing animals.

Most recently one of our cats disappeared when a door was left open. After several weeks with no sign of her I was sure she was killed by a predator. A friend I had made, Amelia Kinkade, is an animal intuitive who lives in Los Angeles. We live in Connecticut and Amelia has never been to our home or near it. I pestered her to tell me where the cat was. She told me in an email, without my even sending Amelia a picture of the cat, "The cat is alive because I can see through its eyes." It detailed the house, yard, other animals and people who were involved in the cat's life. The next day I went out and found the cat exactly where Amelia said it was hiding.

If that doesn't make me a believer about the collective consciousness nothing will. I totally believe that consciousness is non-local and not limited to the body. I also have experienced this through the drawings and dreams of patients I have cared for which allows them to know their diagnosis and what the future holds for them. As Jung said, "The future is unconsciously prepared long in advance and therefore can be guessed by clairvoyants."

I believe it is this unconscious collective awareness that we each are impregnated with when we are born that fuels our lives. So, I do believe that we bring with us the experience of previous lives. Thus the wiser we get the better the future will be for those who follow us.

Bernie Siegel, MD

Introduction

*T*he *Great Joy of Healing Past Lives* can take you on a fascinating journey of personal discovery if:

- you agree with the idea of other lifetimes *or*
- you completely disagree with the idea of other lifetimes *or*
- you are not sure that other lifetimes exist *or*
- you have only a vague feeling that you might have lived before *or*
- you have clear memories of having lived other lifetimes

If past lives are real or simply in our imagination, healing *can occur* by revisiting memories that might be from other lifetimes which we might have lived. There are various methods of revisiting past lives for the purpose of healing. These healing methods, often accompanied by medical and scientific documentation, should no longer be ignored because we can all benefit from the possibility of the resulting physical and emotional health.

The healing method that I use is called EFT, the abbreviation for Emotional Freedom Techniques. EFT is used, often with remarkable results, to help ourselves, our friends and family, animals, even people who we have just met waiting for a flight at the airport or while standing in line at the supermarket. EFT is also used by a growing number of healing professionals. If you are not yet familiar with EFT, you can learn how to apply the basics, for yourself and others, in Chapter 9.

When I use the word *client* in these pages, I am referring to anyone and everyone who can benefit from EFT in any professional or non-professional situation.

In addition, the techniques described throughout *The Great Joy of Healing Past Lives* are many of the same techniques that I use to contact and clear negative events from the past lives of my clients and myself. If you choose to do this work with dedication, integrity and persistent practice, I believe that you will be able to apply these same techniques.

Even though it is not always necessary to look into the distant past to find healing, there are times when the root of a current physical or emotional problem is so thoroughly entwined with another lifetime that real and lasting healing needs to reach that faraway starting place.

Is finding such a past life connection a *difficult* thing to do? Well, it is if you think it is. I have one request for my clients and students in whatever subject they choose to learn from me: please leave the word *difficult* out of your vocabulary. When we tell ourselves that something is *difficult*, guess what happens: it becomes *you-know-what*. Instead, we can replace that nasty word with less limiting choices such as *interesting, fascinating, fun, inspiring, kind of strange, new to me, exciting.* Here's hoping that your vocabulary also helps you benefit from this great world of possibility.

I adopted the theory of reincarnation when I was 26. Genius is experience. Some seem to think that it is a gift or talent, but it is the fruit of long experience in many lives.

HENRY FORD

With Gratitude

I owe my eternal gratitude to Gary Craig, the creator of EFT, for his great courage and persistence in bringing to the world a healing aid as revolutionary as Emotional Freedom Techniques. Although I have never met him personally, the many hours that I have spent studying his work during his actual sessions with EFT clients, have given me a lasting appreciation for his skills, love and dedication. And thank you to his teacher, the late psychologist Dr. Roger Callahan, for being among the first professional healers to successfully combine tapping on the energy system with modern psychology.

I am continually and immeasurably grateful to my amazing husband, Adriano Rosso. His contribution to my life and my work go far beyond the words of any language and well into the feelings gained from his encouragement and love.

And thank you to the dear team who gave so generously of their time to review this work before arriving into your hands:

Dr. Kiya Immergluck is a Pro EFT Master whose wisdom and skills have made a loving contribution to this book. She has been my great pal since childhood, then we went our separate ways, then we re-found each other "coincidently" as EFT Practitioners.

My friend and client, Mina Semyon, first contacted me because she had been diagnosed with glaucoma, a disease that can cause blindness. Inclined to take the alternative route to healing rather than focusing on the disease, she included EFT in her natural health regime. The fact that she was able to read these pages and find my spelling errors is a tribute to the healing of her vision.

Markus Gerber and his brilliant technical expertise, always given willingly from his heart, has also found its way into these pages.

And thank you to my two great Jack Canfield Coaches: Gary Reid with whom I worked for just a few weeks but he made a lasting impression on me with his wisdom and to my coach Wade Lindstrom, his ease in recognizing and celebrating the sweetness of life are treasures beyond measure.

Thank you to my friend Pam Lewis of Nashville for giving me that push of encouragement so many years ago.

My gratitude and appreciation also extends to the good people of Balboa Press as well as to my clients and students for the trust they continue to place in me and their willingness to learn and explore, with me, the marvelous gifts of Energy Healing.

With love and kisses for the inspiration of my children and grandchildren: Senufa, Hiver, Amy, Chris, Tyler, Belinda, Cheyne, Skye, Ronin, Ava and Sophia.

Prelude

When I began to step into distant lifetimes with my EFT clients, the concept was not new to me. I felt I had lived before, but I never talked about it. It was my secret.

Now, as an adult, studying and working in the field of healing, I am happy to know that I am not alone. Some of the great luminaries of our time share my secret, including the psychiatrist Dr. Brian Weiss, who has taken thousands of people back to their other lifetimes for the purpose of healing. A partial list of professionals who publicly embrace the idea of past lives in their work: Gary Craig, Louise Hay, Bruce Lipton, Jack Canfield, Donna Eden, David Feinstein, Barbara Brennan, Gregg Braden, Wayne Dyer and Esther Hicks.

In the pages of *The Great Joy of Healing Past Lives* you will read the personal accounts of some of the sessions I have conducted with EFT clients who have travelled with me into their other lives for the purpose of healing negative situations of this lifetime. Although these stories are all based on fact, I have modified them and changed the names of clients in order to protect their identities and privacy in this subject that can be highly sensitive and controversial for many people.

In selecting the past life EFT sessions to include, I chose examples with diverse approaches in order to give you a variety of ways to enter into and work with past lives – yours and others – for the purpose of healing.

While the energy techniques of EFT (Emotional Freedom Techniques) have produced remarkable documented results, it is a relatively new approach to healing. Neither this book nor EFT can in any way be intended to prevent, diagnose, treat, or cure any physical or psychological illness. The public, therefore, must take complete responsibility for using EFT and the material on the pages of *The Great Joy of Healing Past Lives*. I am not a licensed health care provider. I offer EFT as a personal counselor and teacher. If you are new to tapping, please leave those who are seriously ill to enlightened professionals.

While Gary Craig, the founder of EFT, strongly encourages the worldwide dissemination of EFT, the material in *The Great Joy of Healing Past Lives* includes the interpretations of concepts of EFT that I have written and included in good faith. These interpretations are not necessarily those of Gary Craig.

Minds are like parachutes; they work best when open.

THOMAS DEWAR

Chapter 1

WHAT IS EFT?

*Because of its unique approach, EFT can
work where nothing else does.*

GARY CRAIG
FOUNDER, EFT

EFT stands for Emotional Freedom Techniques. It is a natural, drug-free, gentle and non-invasive system to eliminate the cause of negative emotions that can lead to physical and emotional problems or limit our abilities and talents. Also known as *tapping* or *meridian tapping, Energy Field Tapping, Energy Field Treatment* and *Energy Field Therapy,* EFT is based on the ancient principles and practices of acupuncture but without the use of needles.

Tapping was first introduced in the 1970's by the late clinical psychologist Dr. Roger Callahan in a highly effective method that he called Thought Field Therapy (TFT).

In the 1990's Gary Craig, a student of Dr. Callahan, refined the methods of TFT and became the creator and founder of modern-day EFT. Its use has rapidly spread throughout the world and has been put into practice by hundreds of thousands of non-professionals as well as professionals in various branches of both traditional medicine and alternative health care.

EFT aligns and balances energies in the body through a light tapping with the fingertips on specific points along the meridian pathways of the Energy System. The successes of EFT in rapidly and thoroughly healing physical and emotional problems have made it a modern phenomenon in health care.

When it is correctly applied, EFT works on the real cause of the problem, removing the symptoms of physical or psychological challenges. Even though EFT is often used to clear these problems from our past lives in order to resolve unwanted present situations, the clearing of challenges of other lifetimes is not the focus of EFT.

You can find information on the correct use of EFT in Chapter 9.

In which situations can EFT be of help? Those of us who have experienced benefits from using EFT like to explain it using one of Gary Craig's well known EFT comments, "Try it on everything!"

Here is a partial listing to show you the diverse areas of potential benefits of tapping: stress, depression, insomnia, anxiety, acute pain, chronic pain, allergies anorexia, low self-esteem, excessive shyness, eating disorders, fears and phobias, serious diseases, PTSD (post-traumatic stress disorder), sadness, addictions, anger, test anxiety, weight loss, jealousy, food cravings and many more.

> *EFT is not perfect. We don't get 100%. but it usually works well and the results are sometimes spectacular.*
>
> GARY CRAIG

Chapter 2

HOW CAN YOU KNOW IF YOU HAVE LIVED BEFORE?

According to a Gallup Poll that was done in 2001, twenty-five percent of American adults believe they have lived before [1] and according to a Harris Poll done in 2003, twenty-seven percent of people in the United Kingdom share that belief.[2]

There are various estimates about how many people believe in past lives but it is generally estimated that almost two billion people on Earth believe that they have lived before. Even though that represents about twenty-five percent of the world's population, I did not write *The Great Joy of Healing Past Lives*

---

[1] http://www.gallup.com/poll/4483/"Americans' Belief in Psychic and Paranormal Phenomena Is up Over Last Decade", June 8, 2001

[2] http://www.harrisinteractive.com/vault/Harris-Interactive-Poll-Research, The Harris Poll®,#11,
     "The Religious and Other Beliefs in Britain 2003", February 26, 2003

to try to convince you that you have lived before or that you will live again in another body when you have finished with this one that you now have.

As many as twenty-five per cent of people on Earth believe that our souls are energy bodies that live forever, picking up and letting go of different physical bodies along the way. I cannot say with total proof and scientific certainty that we have had other lifetimes, but polls do indicate that in recent years, more and more people have been embracing the existence of past lives.

What I *do know*, with total certainty, is this: when my EFT clients, students and I use EFT tapping to free ourselves from past life problems, the fears, the pains, the illnesses, the limitations of this lifetime usually improve or completely disappear.

Is it our imagination? I don't think so and I honestly don't care if it is! I am only interested in helping people live better lives in *this* lifetime.

"But", you might be thinking, "is it true that I have lived before?" There are, frankly, many answers to that question and because I encourage you to embrace any skepticism that you might have about past lives, here are some possible explanations:

- Maybe it is true that we are eternal and will live forever picking up different physical bodies along the way and often making the same mistakes over and over again.

- Maybe when people feel that they contact their past lives for therapeutic reasons and they actually do heal problems of their current lives, perhaps something else is taking place that has nothing to do with so-called past lives, also known as "reincarnation".

• Maybe, if reincarnation is a reality, we are like mirrors of ourselves becoming better, wiser, more intelligent or more creative with each life experience or making the same or similar *mistakes* lifetime after lifetime until we *learn* from them.

• Maybe by using EFT or being in a hypnotic state people only think that they have contacted past lives. The reason could be that with these two techniques, EFT or hypnosis, the human mind creates metaphorical and symbolic representations that release negative impulses that actually can heal current problems.

• Maybe, for healing and recovery to take place, the mind needs to imagine fictional past lives that are distant and different in all ways from our present lifetime.

• Maybe the human mind needs to readjust itself and imagine the causes of a current problem to have originated in another lifetime simply because it would be too painful to blame the cause of a current problem on negative circumstances of this lifetime.

• Maybe the answer is that we humans, through EFT or hypnosis, need to by-pass our conscious minds and allow our subconscious to heal us but only when we create past life identities.

The act of contacting our distant past and becoming liberated from misconceptions and limiting beliefs about ourselves can free us from both physical and psychological distortions. The problem is that we humans often tend to carry around a lot of limiting beliefs inside of us, believing that those misconceptions are the truths about ourselves and our world.

Whatever the truth is, the fact that people have been known to revisit what they believe are their past lives and actually feel better and even, by doing so, heal present life problems, is a tribute to the magnificent powers and abilities of the human mind. It is the healing that we, even those who are the most skeptical among us, ought to be celebrating.

Are past lives real or imagined? I vote for past lives!

Of course we are eternal. We have lived before and we will live again; it is only logical.

CHIEN-HAO LIN

Chapter 3

NEW TERMINOLOGY FOR OUR ANCIENT WAYS

Past Life Stress (PLS)
& Past Life Trauma Sequence (PLTS)

I am pleased to introduce two terms that I have coined. An understanding of these simple concepts can help resolve past life trauma that can affect us adversely in this lifetime.

<u>Past Life Stress (PLS)</u>

The word "stress" has become a major part of our modern vocabulary. Hans Selye M.D, Ph.D. first used the word, *stress* in 1936 when he defined it as the "non-specific response of the body to any demand for change."[3]

---

[3]   Hans Selye, MD, PhD *The Stress of Life,* 1956

Today, *stress* is rightfully blamed for an enormous range of problems including pimples, forgetfulness, headaches, heart attacks, cancer and much more.

> "Stress is the body and mind's response to any pressure that disrupts its normal balance… stress is really caused by our emotional reactions to events."
>
> *The Heart Math Institute*

In its most basic functions, stress is not always bad. We humans have been experiencing stress since our prehistoric beginnings when the stress response that took place in our bodies alerted us to the potential danger of any nearby saber-tooth tiger, an approaching dinosaur or similar threat to our safety and wellbeing.

Today, as in the lives of our cave-dwelling ancestors, our built-in system of protection begins with our awareness of danger. The magnificent mechanisms of the mind/body connection immediately send chemicals racing throughout our bodies so that we can respond to the danger and either run from it or fight against it. It is this "fight or flight" response that has been our companion and friend throughout human history.

The prehistoric threat of wild animals lurking in the bushes is no longer a big problem for most of us. *We do have other situations that are potential triggers for the identical fight or flight stress response in our bodies:* we have bills to pay, challenges with our children, worries about our relationships, the economy, lack of self-confidence, the boss at work, our weight, taxes, fears, homework, you name it. We have big stresses and many little stresses that can pile up inside of us.

In essence, the stress response is our way of protection in times of perceived danger. It is, however, often over-worked causing results on our physical and emotional health that can be devastating.

Through the wisdom of modern science we have learned that the fight or flight stress response can harm our bodies when it continues longer than needed for our protection. Its opposite, *the relaxation response*, can support and encourage our health.

It seems that we humans are either in a stress response or in a relaxation response to life. What are we responding to? We are responding to our own thoughts, our environment, our world, our future, our past, to everything and everyone to which we put our attention – either consciously or subconsciously. Many of our thoughts are negative and contain fear, worry, limitations, frustration, hopelessness and all the rest of traditional human negativity. We have become experts at creating our own stress response simply by thinking our negative thoughts.

According to Dr. Herbert Benson[4], cardiologist, and founder of Harvard University's Mind/Body Medical Institute, the relaxation response can counteract the negative physiological effects of the stress response.

The relaxation response can occur in many ways: when we are feeling happy, safe, secure, trusting, loved and loving, living our life purpose, meditating, laughing, and so on.

What does this have to do with past lives? Everything. When we are not experiencing the relaxation response, there is a good possibility that we are under some degree of negative stress. When we have unresolved issues and traumas from the events of our past lives, we can become negatively re-stimulated

---

[4]   Herbert Benson, MD *The Relaxation Response*

by those events without realizing that they might be the real cause of our present physical and/or emotional problems.

Past Life Trauma Sequence (PLTS)

A Past Life Trauma Sequence refers to a sequence of similar events that take place for the same person in various lifetimes. As in working with EFT tapping to clear trauma in *this* lifetime, negative events that contain common elements, such as the punishment of a little boy by a violent father, are often repeated. In this example, the violence that was experienced in the little boy's childhood could condition him as an adult, to subconsciously seek out relationships where he is treated with emotional and/or physical violence.

The little boy's negative and traumatic experiences might, instead, condition him as an adult to commit acts of violence on others or perhaps to work professionally to protect children from violence.

In another example of PLTS, Debra, a client in her mid-50's told me:

> "I feel like I'm a magnet for jerks (she actually used a stronger word than 'jerks'). My relationships start out great and some even stay great for a long time but eventually, every boyfriend I've had ends up either cheating on me or stealing money from me or both. I have always blamed them for their behavior but since it's happened so often, I'm starting to wonder if something about me attracts jerks like them."

In later chapters of *The Great Joy of Healing Past Lives* you will see various methods you can use to contact past lives in order to resolve present problems. In working with Debra, an attractive and intelligent professional woman, I first looked into this lifetime to see if we could find any experiences in her early childhood that might have conditioned her to attract men who ended up as cheaters and robbers.

We found an extremely happy childhood, excellent relationships with schoolmates and supportive professional relationships with colleagues throughout her career. In other words, we found no emotional or physical traumas with any elements that might have conditioned Debra to attract *jerks* into her present adult life.

In looking earlier than her present lifetime, into her distant past, we found some highly traumatic past life experiences with romantic relationships. We found times when she was the perpetrator, involved in her own acts of robbing and cheating people who trusted her. The PLTS definition of trauma includes harmful actions that have been either committed against us as well as harmful actions that we have committed against others.

We also found that for many lifetimes, sometimes as a woman, sometimes as a man, she had made a subconscious decision to remain alone for her own protection from the potential "love pain" of intimate relationships.

In this present lifetime, however, she spent her childhood with a loving family. As the years passed, she found out that her schoolmates all grew up to find loving partners. As an adult, she met professional colleagues who seemed to have perfect romantic relationships. All of this resulted in shifting her earlier decision of remaining alone for her own protection. She began to feel that it was safe to have a relationship.

We worked with EFT to clear away a variety of romantic traumas from her distant past. It became clear to her that, in this lifetime, she had been carrying with her two strong and contradictory decisions: one to remain alone and the other to have a loving relationship just like so many people in her family, her friends and her colleagues had. Did our work together clear the way to bring her a lasting loving relationship with the man of her dreams? Or, on the other hand, is she living a happy and fulfilled life even as a single woman?

It is too soon to know because our work has been fairly recent. She told me, however, that because of the learning she experienced in reviewing some of her past lives, she is now confident that either with a man or as a single woman she will continue to be happy and, most important to her, she feels permanently jerk-free.

The actions of The Law of Attraction can explain this mental phenomenon.

> *The Law of Attraction says: That which is like unto itself, is drawn...**nothing** merely shows up in your experience. You attract it—all of it. No exceptions.*
>
> ESTHER & JERRY HICKS[5]

In doing this work, it seems to me that most of us humans are basically good, kind and caring by nature. When we have done what we perceive to be "bad things" either by committing

---

[5]   Esther & Jerry Hicks *The Law of Attraction; The Basics of the Teachings of Abraham*

harmful acts or by our lack of doing something, for example, to help another, we might feel the results of our behavior as a trauma that remains as an element in our energy system. The unwanted side effects of our past behavior might remain with us until the experience has been resolved and cleared. EFT is an excellent choice for doing that!

In working with clients and myself to heal past life trauma, I often encounter similar negative events in different lifetimes. Being aware of PLTS, we can more easily notice when there are sequences with common aspects. The clearing of these sequences with EFT tapping can bring relief to situations of this lifetime and, I believe, bring a welcomed end to attracting similar negative situations now and in the future.

Sometimes, just the remembrance of past-life traumas leads to incredible insights and healings.

Brian Weiss, MD

Chapter 4

ENERGY

Energy, defined in a non-technical way, is simply *something that is eternal and cannot be created or destroyed.*

For a moment, at least for the length of this chapter, imagine that you and I, everyone you know and every person who lives in this world of ours is made of that energy defined above. If you are more comfortable using another word instead of *energy* feel free to substitute it as you read. Some choices could be *spirit, essence, core, psyche, consciousness, being, higher self* or *soul.*

While you are imagining, think about the concept that we are not bodies that HAVE souls (or spirit, consciousness, etc.) but that we ARE souls that have these *temporary* bodies of ours. These souls that we *are* consist of pure energy and *this* is who we really are.

If we really are pure *energy* and energy cannot be created or destroyed, then we can assume that we are *eternal.* This energy concept is not always the easiest idea for most of us to accept.

Begin to see yourself as a soul with a body
rather than a body with a soul.

WAYNE DYER, PHD

Modern science is making great advances in human knowledge. Information is becoming available to us thanks, in part, to highly sensitive electronic instruments that can measure what we do not detect with our physical senses.

We now know, for example, that the space between physical things is not "nothing". Instead, there is a dynamic and vibrant energy and this energy connects all that is physical. This energy is invisible to the physical senses of most humans yet there is this connection of energy in and between every one of our cells. There is energy in all life. It is in and between bones, muscles, organs and tissues in our bodies. It is in and between parts of plants and animals. It is in and between and connecting us with all the people near us. It is in and between and connecting us with those who are quite far away from us.

And, there is energy between us, our pasts and even our most distant pasts. And when this energy field is merged or combined with the physical body, we can *access* memories through what we call "The Energy System". Parts of this Energy System include the meridians and the tapping points. (Note: In Chapter 9 you will find information about the meridians as well as the tapping points that are used in EFT.)

And so the genius of EFT permits us to be in direct contact, through the tapping points, with all that we are and all that we ever have been. The importance of this contact is to clear away the effects of past negative energy that we have consciously or even subconsciously held onto or accumulated from traumatic experiences. It is also possible, through the gentle stimulation of these tapping points, sometimes known as *acupoints,* to revisit and recover abilities and talents from our past lives and bring them into the present.

The soul comes from without into the human body,
as into a temporary abode, and it goes out of it anew,
passing into other habitations, for the soul is immortal.
RALPH WALDO EMERSON

Energy and Healing

Our energetic system of meridian pathways seems to remember emotional connections that we have made with our past negative experiences. Most of these memories are subconscious. Using EFT, we can unblock those connections, let them go and be free of them.

Those of us who work with this energy field know that the release and clearing of negative energy in this lifetime can create improvements in physical and mental health. In today's medicine, it has become almost common knowledge that the "invisible" forces on the body such as feeling stress or feeling love are capable of having profound impact on our physical health or lack of it.

In much the same way that a twenty-year-old argument can remain with us to cause malfunctions in today's physical body, it also seems to be true that this same negative energy can remain with us throughout many different lifetimes.

In working with EFT and past lives, my clients and I have come to realize that we are somehow a form of this eternal energy. And the energy that we are is in some form of evolution, growing and learning, evolving from lifetime to lifetime. When we honor that idea, respect it, really love it and live the days of this life remembering that this is who we really are, and that it is completely okay that we are eternal, our present lives take on a new and delicious meaning.

We know that negative energy loses its power with EFT tapping. If the negative energy that we tap on is from a traumatic past life event, that event might actually be basic or core to other negative moments that followed it.

It is also possible that we have been attracting similar problems to ourselves because the negative energy of the original trauma has remained in our Energy System.

We also know that we cannot change the negative events of the past. They happened. We can, however, use EFT to change the negative effects that those past events can have on our current physical and/or emotional health, happiness and wellbeing.

Those negative "bad events" might be remembered consciously or unknown to us if they are held in our subconscious memory making it highly possible to have a problem and not have realized its cause. When we are able to use EFT to let go of the real root causes of our problems from either our present or past lives that, I believe, is real freedom.

I think that the only way we can have obstacles working with past lives is when we make it something weird and strange or, even worse, spooky, like something about ghosts. In my experience, this work is nothing like that. My basic feeling is that we really are energy bodies evolving and learning from lifetime to lifetime. When we revisit and clear negative energy from the events of a past life, even if an event includes a past death, we have the opportunity to learn and to evolve. It seems that the death of those we love is probably worse for those of us who miss them; they are okay.

This work is *not* about death – it *is*, instead, about life and living free from unwanted negative baggage from our past and distant past.

When the actress, Lilli Palmer asked the blind woman, Helen
Keller, *"Do you believe in life after death?"*
Miss Keller replied emphatically:
*"Most certainly! It is no more than passing from one
room to another but there's a difference for me, you know,
because in that other room I shall be able to see."*
CANFIELD, HANSEN, HAWTHORNE & SHIMOFF
*A SECOND CHICKEN SOUP
FOR THE WOMAN'S SOUL*

∼✦✧∼

*...I do know that each cell, organ, system
of organs and person is directed by what I
call the loving intelligence of energy.*

BERNIE SIEGEL, MD
PEACE, LOVE & HEALING

∼✦✧∼

Chapter 5

USING EFT TO HEAL
PAST LIVES

In my work as an EFT Practitioner, I prefer to help my clients find resolution to their presenting problems by first looking for the causes of their problems in this lifetime. I only refer to past lives when we are not able to find resolution after a thorough search in this life.

The simple reason that I would rather look into this lifetime first is because this life has its limitations. Clients know when and where they were born. They know if they were born a girl or boy. Many details of their current lives are readily available.

When a problem remains after doing what feels like a thorough job of looking for its cause in this lifetime without results, I look to past lives. The beautiful thing about this is that it does not seem to matter if the traumas that happened in the past lives that we work on and clear with EFT are, for the client, *real or symbolic or imagined.*

Once we start looking into their other lifetimes for the cause of a current problem, there are unlimited possibilities. What were the circumstances when the bad event happened? Was the person a man or a woman? Was the person a child or adult? What country did she or he live in? Were the events of a certain past life the cause of the present problem or were they only similar, such as in PLTS, keeping the original trauma stimulated life after life?

When people contact me because they are curious or just want to know if they lived before, I would not take on that person as a client. My only reason for working with past lives is to help clear away present problems with EFT.

I could well imagine that I might have lived in former centuries and there encountered questions I was not yet able to answer; that I had been born again because I had not fulfilled the task given to me.

CARL JUNG

My past life clients are in six different categories; you will find examples of these categories throughout the book. These are real stories about Life itself.

Past Life Session Categories

1. Believer Clients
   They know they have lived before or just have a feeling that they did. When I suggest the idea of looking into

another lifetime with such a client, there is usually instant agreement and the response will be something like, "Sure, Judy, let's try that!"

It *does* happen but it is unusual to have that kind of immediate interest in exploring the events of a past life as a cause of a current problem.

When the idea of past lives *is* accepted by a client as real or at least possible, the work itself is simply straightforward EFT. The *only* difference is that the specific events that we clear happened during another lifetime and so we can move fairly quickly to clearing the Past Life Stress.

2. Skeptical Clients

    This group is resistant and skeptical to the idea of past lives. They feel it is absolutely impossible to have lived before. That is when I need to approach my work differently using metaphors or symbols.

3. Automatic Clients

    The automatic group arrives at an event of a past life automatically while working on an event of this lifetime. The past life event simply arrives by itself while we are tapping. This can happen even when someone does not believe in past lives.

    When it happens, I simply follow them to the troublesome past life memory and work to clear it with EFT.

4. Clue-Giver Clients

    Clients often give us 'clues' to unlocking the information of a negative event even when that information is not readily available in their conscious thoughts.

    Gary Craig refers to those moments as part of "The Art of EFT". Practitioners need to be extremely alert and work at an expert level in order to notice even the slightest change of a client's expression, body movement or choice of words. These subtle changes might lead to contacting and clearing a key negative experience in either this or another lifetime.

5. Child Clients

    Depending on their individual situations, children usually make relatively fast progress with standard EFT. When I feel the need to look into the possibility of another lifetime with a child, I treat the session as a standard session without discussing past lives.

6. Ourselves

    One of the many beautiful things about EFT is the ability to help ourselves with our own life problems and to enhance our own talents and abilities.

    ... They are, as I realized in my flash of insight while mulling over the mechanics of the cellular membrane – immortal, as I believe we all are.

    BRUCE LIPTON, PHD
    THE BIOLOGY OF BELIEF

Chapter 6

MEASURING THE RESPONSE OF ENERGY

In EFT, we look for the aspects, or elements, of troublesome past specific events that have occurred and caused problems for the client. Why do we do this? Because those events usually remain in the human Energy System as stored electric negative energy referred to by Gary Craig as *zzztts*. These *zzztts*, when left in our Energy System, can cause or contribute to a long and varied list of unwanted physical, emotional and mental problems.

The events that have created the *zzztts* are either remembered consciously or not remembered if they are stored in the client's subconscious memory. With the techniques of EFT, there is a great probability of clearing away the effects of both conscious and subconscious negative energy, giving the client endless possibilities for health, happiness and freedom from the troublesome, traumatic and limiting *zzztts*.

It is estimated by many experts that only approximately five percent of human memory is available as conscious thought while approximately nine-five percent is stored in our subconscious and is not readily available to us. [6]/[7]

As an adult, you might easily remember the color of your kitchen walls when you were five years old; that information is stored as a conscious memory if there was no trauma associated with your kitchen. If, however, a stray dog entered the kitchen and frightened you when you were five, you might not easily remember the color of the kitchen walls. You might not even remember that dog because the event in the kitchen was a traumatic experience for you. As an adult, you might also be afraid of dogs without knowing the reason for your fear.

Our subconscious minds have been wonderfully designed to carry out complicated and vital functions for us. It is the subconscious that has a key role in our beating hearts because we do not need to consciously count "one heartbeat, two heartbeats....." in order for our hearts to keep on beating. So many functions of life in our bodies take place without the slightest conscious thought, from the blinking of our eyes to the releasing of digestive enzymes. Our subconscious can also protect us by blocking out, from our conscious memory, traumatic events from either the recent or the distant past.

---

[6]   Bruce Lipton, PhD; author *The Biology of Belief,* published by Hay House

[7]   Gary Craig, *The EFT Manual*

The intuitive mind is a sacred gift and the rational mind is a faithful servant. We have created a society that honors the servant and has forgotten the gift.

ALBERT EINSTEIN

Three Methods of Locating Specific Events

I have learned to trust my own intuition while doing both this lifetime as well as past life work. I have also learned to trust the intuition of my clients. I find, however, that the work can move smoother and quicker when I also use certain instruments and methods to measure the energetic response of clients, during EFT sessions, while they are focused on conscious memories, subconscious impressions and feelings or on my specific questions.

If a client does not remember the date or other details of a traumatic event, which needs to be released from the person's subconscious memory in order to be free of its negative effects in the present and future, I can safely and gently use these techniques to find the information. In past life work it is often helpful to know the century or lifetime in which the bad thing happened. These methods also give clients the unique opportunity of observing the energetic response of the instruments for themselves.

In using one or all of the following techniques, it is important to be objective in not having pre-determined decisions about the cause of a client's problem. The same applies when we are working on ourselves. It is not always easy to be objective as we have many years of experience in forming our own observations, opinions and judgments.

In doing this work, our intuition needs to be separate and different from opinion and judgment in order to remain objective. One of the best ways that I have found to free myself from the limitations that come with not being objective is the practice of meditation. The meditation practice that I often use and teach is called *"mindful meditation"*. It was created by Jon Kabat-Zinn, PhD.[8]

Meditation is not a way of making your mind quiet. It is a way of entering into the quiet that is already there, buried under the 50,000 thoughts the average person thinks every day.

DEEPAK CHOPRA, MD

Meditation, a practice I recommend highly, is another basic method for opening up your awareness to past life memories.

BRIAN WEISS, MD

There are many excellent approaches and methods of meditation; the reasons I recommend mindful meditation, also known as mindfulness, are that it is easy to learn and to use. Mindfulness is highly effective in bringing ourselves into the

---

[8]   Jon Kabat.Zinn, PhD, *Mindfulness for Beginners: Reclaiming the Present Moment--and Your Life*

present moment.[9] If you are already a meditator and you use a method that you enjoy and that brings you into the present "now", continue enjoying what works best for you.

One of the most fundamental teachings of EFT is that it goes "through" us and is not done "by" us. When we let EFT move through us, with clients or ourselves, we will often have the spectacular results for which EFT is so famous.

When, on the other hand, we let our egos lead the way with the idea that we are responsible for the healing, quite possibly the results will be limited or non-existent. How do we learn to let EFT go *through* us? I believe it might be easier when we know how to meditate. Is meditation a requirement to doing successful EFT for this or past lifetimes? No, it isn't. But as both my Lithuanian and Russian grandmothers used to say about other matters, "It wouldn't hurt!"

Once we have experienced this eternal part in us,
we can no longer doubt its existence. Meditation is
thus the way to knowing and beholding the eternal,
indestructible, essential center of our being.

RUDOLF STEINER

I also use and teach my students and clients to use one or a combination of the three following methods to measure energetic response. The use of whichever of these methods is most comfortable for you and your clients is an excellent guide to selecting which one to use. I sometimes combine methods

---

9   Shamash Alidina, *Mindfulness for Dummies*

as they are outstanding tools in locating various aspects to help clear the repeated triggers of the PLTS:

1. *Applied Kinesiology, also known as Muscle-Testing*

   Applied Kinesiology (kə-nee'see-ŏl'ə-gee) was created by the American chiropractor, Dr. George Goodheart, in the 1960's; it is a gentle, safe, non-invasive technique with no negative side effects. [10]

   Muscle-testing is easily used as a method of identifying how energy is moving in the physical body. Along with many practitioners in this field, I often use applied kinesiology to measure energetic response to my questions and comments while my clients and I are looking for the aspects of specific negative events to clear with EFT.

   In addition to clearing away the negative, we can also use these methods to locate and enhance past skills and abilities such as the creativity of artistic and performance talents.

   Applied Kinesiology (muscle-testing) is very simple to use. If you do not yet know how to use it there are classes and seminars, books and YouTube videos. Please see the Resource Section at the end of *The Great Joy of Healing Past Lives* for some suggestions.

---

[10]   Roger J. Callahan, PhD, *The Five-Minute Cure for Public Speaking and Other Fears*

When I muscle test a client or student, I use the basic technique of applying slight pressure to the person's extended arm. You can see this technique on many YouTube videos. In teaching my students and clients to use healing methods for themselves, their families and friends, several methods for self-administered muscle-testing, while applying slight pressure to the fingers, work very well. You can also see these self-administered muscle-testing methods demonstrated on YouTube videos. If you do not have a computer with Internet capabilities, you can always find a friend, public library, Internet café or store with Internet that you can easily use for a small fee or sometimes without charge.

In addition to intuition and muscle-testing, I often use the following two instruments to measure energetic response for the purpose of locating the content of specific negative events in a client's past as well as finding repeated aspects found in a PLTS.

I know very well that many scientists consider dowsing as a type of ancient superstition. According to my conviction this is, however, unjustified. The dowsing rod is a simple instrument which shows the reaction of the human nervous system to certain factors which are unknown to us at this time.

ALBERT EINSTEIN

2. *Dowsing with The Pendulum*

Pendulums have probably been used as "tools" to measure unseen energy since the beginning of time. It is not actually known how long humans have been using pendulums but they certainly have a long history. The first recorded used of pendulums was in the Orient more than 5,000 years ago.

The Pendulum

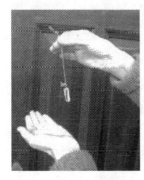

Note the slightly angular movement of the pendulum as I hold it over my open hand. It was actually moving in a circular motion when the photo was taken.

The use of pendulums is also known as *radiesthesia* or *dowsing*. If you are not yet skilled at using pendulums, you can learn to use them to measure the subtle energies emitted by any living source human, animal or plant. We can also use pendulums to find lost objects or to locate underground water.

In considering the purchase of our home and farm in Italy several years ago, I used my pendulum to learn if there was really needed water under the ground as the real estate sales agents had assured us. Even though I personally believed that there was water and the real estate agents were quite convincing that water existed, the response from the pendulum was a definite "NO!" to my question about the existence of water. As

31

a result, we did not buy that house and the absence of water in that property was later confirmed.

If you do not yet use a pendulum, it is easy to learn. For some people the ability to use a pendulum arrives immediately. For others it takes some practice to make a connection between one's energy and the correct response of the instrument. It is easiest for meditators to make that connection because they can calm their own thoughts and be objective when they do the testing.

Pendulums can be made of anything from a pretty crystal to a pine cone on a string. You can make your own or buy one. In an emergency situation that I had when I did not have a pendulum with me, I had excellent results using a used teabag on a string! You can find all the information you need about how to make or buy a pendulum on the Internet and in books. If, in your research about making and using pendulums, you find some contrasting ideas, I suggest that you simply follow the ideas that feel right to you and use your own intuition.

Dowsing is a way in which our subconscious produces micro movements so that our conscious can be aware of it.

WILLIAM TILLER, PH.D.

3. *The Bio-Tensor*

Bio-tensors function basically in the same ways as pendulums. There are many different types of bio-tensors. The type and material you use depends only on your personal preference.

The Bio-Tensor

This is a photo of my bio-tensor,
it is made entirely of metal.
Bio-tensors are also available with
wooden or crystal handles and in
a variety of ring styles and materials.

Learning to use the bio-tensor correctly is more complex than using the pendulum. You can find a lot of information about them on the Internet and in books but I suggest that if you want to be proficient in their use, study with a bio-tensor expert. Even though there are many uses of bio-tensors, I use mine to help find out specific information about the content of specific negative events in order to help clear those events with EFT.

Which is the Best Instrument to Use?

Between the pendulum and bio-tensor, I use the instrument with which an individual client is most comfortable. Sometimes I use both in order to verify a client's response to a question. If a new client feels that I am manipulating a pendulum or bio-tensor, I would ask the person to hold the instrument while the questions are asked and answered.

In later chapters, I will share with you some actual examples of using pendulums and bio-tensors with clients.

There are two guiding principles for proper use of these instruments:

1. Always use them ethically.
2. Avoid asking questions for information about the future.

As you will see in the following chapter, my questions are only about the past and/or present.

Most of my clients and students have their own instruments. Some have told me that they do not use the instruments because they feel that they influence 'yes' or 'no' *answers* with their own thoughts. The mere fact, however, that someone could mentally influence such movement is a great tribute to the huge power of the mind.

I suggest that a solution to receiving correct information is to practice a lot with things you already know as true. For example, ask if the table in front of you is a table or if it is an elephant. I usually ask clients to do homework between our EFT sessions. Homework may include using the pendulum, bio-tensor or muscle-testing for themselves. The homework is not usually about past lives but is often based on Gary Craig's "Personal Peace Procedure" (see Resource Section).

MEASURING THE RESPONSE OF ENERGY

Live so that you may desire to live again; that is your duty for in any case you will live again.

FRIEDRICH NIETZSCHE

Chapter 7

PAST LIFE EFT SESSIONS

The following are examples of experiences I have had with clients and how I have used EFT to clear traumas from their other lifetimes. Every time I have the opportunity of traveling with clients back into times and places, I feel as though they are telling and re-telling our human story. It's a story with a profound range of depths, colors, traditions and so many ideas, opinions and viewpoints from which to see and know the world and life's great contrast and diversity.

Working in this way with clients, or with ourselves, often means to move on, going from being a victim who has been carrying the often horrendous effects of a long-forgotten subconscious traumatic tragedy to becoming more alive.

Resistance to the Idea of Past Lives

I have had clients who, at first, were resistant to the subject of past lives. Some have been vehemently resistant while others find the possibility of living before to be funny, silly or completely ridiculous; they absolutely do not believe in past lives. This is an example of The Category 2, Skeptical Client, mentioned in Chapter 5.

Yet, on the other hand, they want to resolve a specific emotional or physical problem which, up until now, has not been completely handled or improved, either by me using standard "this lifetime" EFT, or by any number of therapists or medical physicians or specialists.

I always tell resistant clients that although I have personally experienced benefits in past life work for myself as well as other clients, I will not bring up the subject with them again. Furthermore, if they do ever want to discuss past life work with me, I will be happy to answer any questions but they will need to be the ones who initiate any past life discussion.

We know it is always important to establish rapport with clients and patients and to do what we can for them to feel safe with us. This is *extremely* true when entering into the subject of past lives. I always, even with clients with whom I've worked many times, remind them again that they are free to stop the session at any time and for whatever reason of their own choosing. Also, if they don't want me to know something too personal, they can always say something like, "hmm hmm hmm" while they privately focus mentally on the actual situation, as Gary Craig taught us to do with standard EFT. [11]/[12]

---

[11]   Gary Craig, *The EFT Manual*

[12]   Judith Rivera Rosso, *EFT & Life eBook*

This work does not force clients to look into another lifetime for answers and resolution to a current problem. The work is about respect; it is not about force. It is similar to the fact that we can often use EFT to help someone stop smoking but we cannot convince or cajole a smoker to try EFT to give up the habit without his or her desire to stop smoking.

In those situations where there is any level of resistance to the idea of past lives but where there is the client's interest in resolving the problem, the first thing we do is to create a symbol or a metaphor for their problem. In doing that, I feel it is critical to the success of the session to establish a foundation of certainty for them that I am not going to, in any way, ask them to remember or even think about, the possibility of living before.

One of my first experiences working with someone's past life was one of my most resistant past life clients. The session took place six years ago.

I had, in the past, successfully treated her with EFT for a health problem. She is a very quiet and shy lady who lives in a nearby village. When she arrived for her appointment she told me that she had recently celebrated her 50th birthday and that for her entire life she felt inferior to men.

She added that she was sometimes afraid of men, never completely comfortable around them, not even at the dinner table with her husband of many years and their two adult sons. She always accepted that feeling afraid and uncomfortable was just the way she was. But when she turned 50, and after overcoming a big problem with EFT, she wondered if she could finally get over her fear of men, too.

We had worked on her earliest memories of this lifetime during two sessions and although she received other benefits, the fear of men did not go away. When I suggested that we could try to look into her past lives for the cause of these feelings, she almost ran out of my studio. "But, Judy, that's against my religion!" she said.

I, of course assured her that I would never do anything against her religion. I told her that I would like to try another approach to see if we could resolve this problem. She agreed and scheduled another session.

This time, I tapped on her continuously and slower than usual. I find this is very relaxing. I asked her to close her eyes and keep them closed and to pretend, to imagine a big pink cloud underneath her, holding her up in the air, while she was very relaxed. When I could see that she was relaxed, I asked her to let her thoughts fly away. I spoke quietly and slowly. I asked her to make her mind the color white and to breathe gently. I asked her to *pretend*, to *imagine* what could happen to *another* person — to a woman or to a girl or to a man, or to a little child, to make someone feel exactly the way *she* feels about men.

I had been tapping slowly and gently for ten or twelve minutes when she suddenly moved back in her chair, reacting to something. Continuing to speak softly, I asked her to keep her eyes closed and tell me what was happening.

She said that she imagined feeling like someone who was closed inside a cage and that the cage was on the ground, in a forest. As she spoke, she began to cry. I continued tapping gently and only saying, very quietly sometimes *"...ah hah, tell me more...."* I usually speak very quietly when I do this work;

sometimes I even whisper to help keep the person's attention on the past negative event that we are working to clear away.

She said that the only thing she could see were men's feet in leather bags, like old shoes, made by hand, like in medieval days. She said things like, *"This is so sad...this is a terrible trap..."* She muttered and whispered things to herself. I could not understand all her words so I followed my own intuition about what she was saying and I said things like, *"Even though this person is in a cage, trapped by these men, she deserves her freedom...she is trapped by the men and they are wrong, this cage is so small, she deserves to be free... she was trapped then, now she is free."* I continued applying EFT while speaking quietly and slowly tapping, with reminder phrases such as *"... she is trapped by those men...the cage is so small...this fear she feels...this fear of those men...she was trapped by those men...those men were wrong...she deserves to be free...now she is free..."*

After many rounds of tapping very slowly and lightly, I asked her to imagine the freedom this person in the cage wanted. I asked her to feel that freedom deep inside herself now and all over her body. To feel freedom for this person deep in her own heart now. To feel free in every cell of her own body now, in her arms and legs, in her muscles and tendons, in her jaws. I asked her to imagine opening that cage from the inside just by blowing softly on the door. And she did it. The cage opened for her and she was free from the men in the forest who held her captive. All this happened, of course, in the mind of my client.

She opened her eyes on her own. She was shaking a little. Physical shaking is often a natural and automatic response done to release the "freeze response"[13] of trauma. I didn't say anything to her about the shaking. She was also smiling a little and I realized then that I had never seen her smile before. She didn't want to talk about anything. She wiped her tears. She thanked me. She hugged me. She paid me for the session and said she needed to leave. She said that she wanted to make a nice dinner for her family. She was smiling all the time.

The length of that session was much longer than the time it has taken you to read this account. Up until this point, we were in session for approximately 90 minutes.

Now, I would like to ask you a question: what do you think was happening in the mind of my client? Was she imagining the events she described or was she remembering them? Were the cage, the men, the forest and the sad feeling of being trapped by men wearing medieval footwear all in her imagination? Or, did she contact a memory from a past life?

Neither you nor I and, perhaps not even my client, can really answer those questions beyond what we feel or believe actually happened during that session. The only thing I can be certain of is that by tapping on her Energy System with EFT, while she focused on a negative event of her own choosing, she was able to be free from years of emotional limitations and fears.

Based on the fact that I have had many similar experiences working with clients and with my own experiences, I am of the opinion that in this session the lady contacted a past life. The clearing of her negative and highly traumatic past life experience that occurred during the session resulted in positive benefits by accomplishing her original intention.

---

[13]   Robert Scaer, MD, *The Body Bears the Burden: Trauma, Disassociation and Disease, 2007*

My client and I have never spoken about that session that we had six years ago, but when I saw her the next time after our last session, she was walking in her village. When she saw me, she was "all smiles" and very happy. She hugged me and even winked at me! It was a wink that seemed to say that we both shared a secret and that all was well in her world. Over the years, she and her husband have been taking vacations together and I am happy to report that I have even seen them strolling together, hand in hand.

In our EFT session, *the other person* was an obvious back door approach to the possibility of another life without offending the beliefs of my client. I call it *"The Feel As If Technique"*. Using the idea of the pink cloud underneath, holding her up in the air, helped her relax while I was tapping slowly on her points. *Imagining* another person who was feeling the same fear that she felt about men gave her the direction she needed in beginning to resolve her own fear of men.

Even with clients who were, at first, skeptical to the idea of past lives, in my work there has never been any resistance to the past life idea once the client's information from his or her distant past begins to arrive.

As we live through thousands of dreams in our present life, so is our present life only one of many thousands of such lives.

LEO TOLSTOY

Bill Felt He Lived Before

With clients who are interested in their past lives, the entrance into specific events is easier. Bill was a Category 1, Believer Client, described in Chapter 5. I will call him Bill. He came to me for help with a problem he had for 12 years. He was now 30 years old; the problem began on the day of his high school graduation. He described that day as "a wonderful day". He said that the sun was shining. His parents were there and he was with many friends.

During our first session, Bill told me that when he was in high school, he got along well with most of his teachers but he had serious conflicts with one of them. On the day of his graduation, he remembered some of those conflicts but with a sense of relief that the teacher could no longer exert any power over him. He referred to that teacher as "evil, vicious and terrifying".

Bill said that during the graduation ceremony, his hands and arms began shaking for no reason. He tried to stop the shaking but the more he tried, the stronger the shaking became. He was concluding his high school years and looking forward to college. All was well in his world and, looking back, he told me that he saw no reason for his hands and arms to shake.

In his youth, he had dreams of becoming an acupuncturist. During the past twelve years, the shaking continued and those dreams disappeared. He knew that the delicate work with needles that acupuncture requires was not possible without steady hands and arms. He had tried many different physical, mental and stress-related therapies to resolve the problem but without a cure or even a diagnosis for the shaking.

He complained of having many years of embarrassing moments, problems in his social life, even the inability to hold a glass of wine or cup of coffee without spilling the contents. He felt himself withdrawing from life and was still living with his family because he was unable to support himself.

I began our first session by tapping on issues of this lifetime, including all things connected with his high school experiences and the graduation. We spent the remainder of our first session clearing some problems that were unrelated to the tremors. In our second session, we continued working on issues of this lifetime including his childhood, his infancy, his birth and even his time spent in the womb before his birth.

Bill was experiencing definite benefits from EFT, but, so far, nothing had improved with his tremors. I asked him how he felt about the idea of having lived before in past lives. His response was positive and so we began our first past life EFT session.

Sometimes I tap directly on my clients. When clients tap on themselves, I usually tap on myself at the same time with them. There are two primary reasons that I also tap: one, so that clients, even if highly involved in the personal work of the session can follow the tapping points if their eyes are open. The second reason is that I have the responsibility of maintaining my own free-flowing energy in the best interests of my clients. Clients often tap with their eyes closed and if needed, I say the tapping points out loud to help them know where to tap.

Intention in the Past Life Session

I began by saying what I often say at the start of EFT sessions by asking Bill, while he was continually tapping more gently and slower than usual on the side of his hand, to *think about* or *feel* or *have the sensation* of what he wants to gain from the session. I wanted to know what his exact intention was for the session. He told me about some of his intentions and then we talked about them while we both continued slowly tapping on the sides of our hands.

As sometimes happens when I ask the question about a client's intention for the session, he mentioned a few different things that he wanted to accomplish: to stop shaking, to know the reason for his shaking and to overcome a list of additional thoughts and feelings. I believe it is important to have a clear and singular intention because during past life sessions, it is common for many different aspects of specific negative events to be remembered. I often work as a coach before beginning EFT sessions to help clients refine and clarify their purpose for the session. I am more able to guide the client to resolution of the problem when there is a clear and unconfused intention.

For this first past life session, Bill's intention was to know, without any doubt, the cause of the tremors. Another person in his situation might have had the intention of eliminating the shaking but for reasons of Bill's particular individual personality, he wanted more than anything, to know *the reason*. He felt that in knowing the "why" he could heal.

I had used the bio-tensor in previous sessions with Bill and he requested that I use it for past life work with him. I usually suggest that clients have their eyes open when I use the bio-tensor or pendulum. Once we locate a specific event for tapping, I ask them to close their eyes. With eyes closed it is easier to remain focused on the event itself without distractions of the present environment.

Clients with whom I have previously worked often have their eyes closed while I use the bio-tensor or pendulum; they are already familiar with the responses of the instruments. After one or two sessions, they have gained trust in me so that if I tell them that the instrument agrees or disagrees with a specific date in the past, even though they do not see it for themselves, they trust my interpretation of the instrument.

It is important that both the client and I are very relaxed during the session. If I notice the client becoming anxious, I ask about it and, if needed, we tap on the anxiety until he or she is once again relaxed. I always tell clients that they are free to stop the session at any time they want and for whatever reason.

Also, I always remind clients in either this life or past life work that anything they say to me is strictly confidential. In addition, I always tell them that if they come across anything that is too personal to say to me, they do not need to say it. They can simply do as Gary Craig teaches in standard EFT and say something like "hmm hmm hmm" while they are mentally focused on the personal situation and continue tapping. The reason for the "hmm hmm hmm" is to help the person have a sort of 'mental anchor' and remain with the work while tapping instead of drifting off to other thoughts.

I asked Bill to let me know if any impressions came up during the session. For example, if he "sees" a tree or he feels as though he is running, to please let me know even if his impressions make no sense to him. I also ask clients to tell me if they hear or smell something that make no sense to them. Unless clients have the security that it is safe to say such things, they might worry that maybe it is just their imagination or something silly and have doubts that the impression might be a reality from their past. When I know about such impressions, we can verify them with the pendulum, bio-tensor, muscle-testing or all three!

I then told Bill that I would be asking him some questions but that I did not want him to answer me with words. Instead, I would be asking his subconscious directly because it has been recording everything since the beginning of his existence. I asked him if that would be okay and he agreed.

I always first ask the client's subconscious if it is okay for me to ask it questions for the benefit of the client. Bill watched the bio-tensor and observed that its movement was in an up-and-down direction that meant "yes".

I asked Bill's subconscious if it was okay to know the cause of his shaking hands and arms. The response – yes.

I asked if the cause was in this lifetime. The response – no.

If the response had been "yes" to my question about this lifetime, I would have looked again for a possible cause of the tremors in this life in case I missed something in earlier sessions. We want to arrive, when possible, at the cause or core of a problematic situation to find resolution. In tapping, we often take away what seem to be layers of the problem before arriving at its actual cause or core. If you think of the layers as those of an onion, the process is easy to understand.

At the start of past life sessions, both the client and I usually tap on the Karate Chop (KC) point which is located at the sides of our hands or we gently rub one or both of our Sore Spots (SS) (Chapter 9). When I feel a client's need to arrive at a deeper level of relaxation in order to access information from the past, I often ask the person to gently squeeze the sides of their fingertips, one at a time.

Here are some of the other questions that I normally ask while the instrument is engaged. I asked these questions of Bill while he tapped slowly on the side of his hand, with an eye on the bio-tensor for either confirmation or negation:

In the lifetime when the event occurred that began this problem with your shaking hands and arms –

> *Were you a man?* The response – no
> *Were you a woman?* The response – yes
> *Were you a child?* The response – no
> *Were you a baby?* The response – no

As you noticed, I continued asking questions even when he answered "yes" to the second question. The reason to continue is only to test the responses. Sometimes I ask silly test questions such as, *Were you an automobile?*

I also check with the client by asking, *Does it feel right to you that, in the lifetime when the event occurred that began this problem with your shaking hands and arms, you were a woman?*

Bill's response was affirmative.

I then asked for the country where the bad event happened. I usually say several countries until there is an affirmative response or I might ask the client if the country is known to him or her, always tapping slowly and gently on the side of the hand while watching the response of the instrument.

In Bill's case, he knew the country right away. In fact, he said, "I feel like I'm there".

I did not need to ask additional questions to find the specific event in Bill's distant past because he was already "there". If he would not have realized the event so quickly I would have continued with additional questions such as:

How many years ago did the bad event happen that caused the shaking in your hands and arms? or
What was the date of the bad event? or
How many lifetimes ago did the bad event happen?

Once we have established the basic information of the bad event, I stop using the bio-tensor. Any of the methods of energetic measurement can certainly be used during sessions but I prefer to use them only to arrive at the specific event. The remainder of sessions is standard EFT, looking for specific information to tap on and clear away.

I then asked Bill to tell me about the event as I tapped slowly and gently on his tapping points. He told of being in England, in a village, 500 years ago, being tried for some kind of sorcery. In describing the situation, there were judges in front of the young woman who he was. There were also many people standing to her right and to her left. In this memory, she was standing in the middle of these groups of people, on a

THE GREAT JOY OF HEALING PAST LIVES

low platform. Her hands had been mutilated as punishment and there was memory of a lot of pain.

As Bill told his story, I was reminded about how he described the day of his high school graduation in this lifetime in Italy. The teachers were in front of him, families on one side and fellow students on his other side with him as the graduating student, standing in the middle of everyone on a low platform to receive his diploma.

I tapped for many rounds on the various aspects of this highly negative event from Bill's distant past. I also used the advanced EFT technique of Matrix Re-imprinting, (see Resource Section). I began to include aspects of his high school graduation in the Set Up and Reminder Phrases and we tapped on the similarities of these two events – the event of 500 years ago in England and his high school graduation 12 years ago in Italy.

We returned to the event in the U.K. in two following sessions and Bill's tremor improved by about eighty percent. As of this writing, he has enrolled in a school of Chinese medicine where he will be studying acupuncture. Obviously the emotional and physical pains of the trial, judgment and torture he faced in another lifetime were restimulated by the similar surroundings of his graduation ceremony.

All of us probably bring into this lifetime some bad events from our distant past. What, if anything, can we do to stay free and un-restimulated from any subconscious negativity that can creep into an otherwise happy and peaceful experience such as Bill's graduation day?

Preventing Negative Past Life Re-Stimulations in Daily Life

Imagine a sunny day. If you like sunny days imagine having one of them in a place that you like such as a peaceful beach or in the mountains or in a big exciting city. The reason I am asking you to begin this exercise by imagining a sunny day is because it is a metaphor for a good experience, such as the one that Bill had during his high school graduation ceremony.

Then, imagine that in our metaphor the sky turns very dark in the distance and darkness quickly moves closer to you with so much thunder and lightning that one thing becomes obvious: your sunny day is changing.

In this metaphorical example, you have many choices. You could feel miserable because the dark skies of a storm are covering your sunshine. You could stay where you are and get wet. You could be angry and curse the storm. You could have a sense of understanding that the storm is a necessary part of weather on earth. You would have many choices about how you could react to the change in the weather.

And so, Bill's sunny day graduation ceremony changed into a "dark storm" when his hands and arms began to involuntarily shake. On that day, Bill did not have any solutions on how to help himself in that moment.

I am suggesting in this little first aid exercise that when unexplained upsets arrive in our lives, there is a strong possibility that something or someone in our present environment has stimulated a negative subconscious memory. It could be a memory from earlier in this lifetime or from our distant past. When you find yourself feeling badly without any apparent reason, try this little exercise by consciously putting yourself more into the present moment.

If you are not able to do a proper meditation session to put yourself back in the present moment, you can always focus consciously on your breathing. You can consciously feel your feet on the floor and your back on the chair if you are sitting down. You can consciously listen to the sounds around you, including you own heartbeat. If the situation permits, you can walk around and touch things like tables and chairs and walls in your immediate environment while you consciously focus on any difference in the temperature or texture of the furniture.

> *If an Asiatic asked me for a definition of Europe, I should be forced to answer him: 'It is that part of the world which is haunted by the incredible delusion that man was created out of nothing, and that his present birth is his first entrance into life'.*
>
> ARTHUR SCHOPENHAUER

Jack Canfield's 'Yellow Alerts'

Jack Canfield is an extraordinary motivational coach. He is also an EFT tapper. In his teachings, he talks about the idea that life can give us warnings which he calls "yellow alerts", like the yellow alert warnings of the "Star Trek" television programs. If we pay attention to these warnings and do something to improve the situation, we can probably prevent the yellow alert from becoming a more serious "red alert".

If Bill would have known about the possibility that his tremor had something to do with a previous bad experience and if he then would have consciously brought himself totally into the present moment of his graduation ceremony, he might have prevented twelve years of suffering from his severe tremors. Can we know this to be true? Of course not. But you can certainly try this little first aid idea if you get a sudden headache or if you're feeling fine and then you find yourself feeling afraid. The next time your "sunny day" turns dark, see for yourself if you can find relief by putting yourself back into the present moment.

I actually have my own unproven pet theory that eating something that is excessively sweet or salty, when we are not hungry, might be a subconscious attempt to return us back into the present moment. It's just a theory. ☺

Jim Improved His Vision

Jim is a man in his late 30's. I had worked with him previously for glaucoma. Because of his past life experiences with EFT and me, Jim was now a Category 1 Believer Client described in Chapter 5.

The pressure and limitations in his vision from glaucoma have never returned thanks to EFT. He did not become blind as was predicted by specialists over a seven-year period. He was contacting me now because he wanted to make an appointment for a problem in focusing his vision for extended periods of time. This was another vision problem, different from the glaucoma.

When he called me he said that he had been doing his own tapping and was very happy with his progress. He had started to tap, however, on an event that took place when he was nine years old, in this lifetime. He said he could not contact or see all of his nine-year-old self in order to clear an event with EFT and that it was very frustrating for him. We made an appointment.

When Jim arrived, I used the bio-tensor while asking some preliminary "test questions" and checking the yes or no movement of the instrument. I often ask clients to tell me their name or the country we are in as we watch the movement of the bio-tensor or pendulum or feel the muscle strength when using kinesiology. I also ask clients to lie to me and tell me, with certainty, that they have another name or that we are in another country. I always use the test questions at the start of every session, including my own sessions.

It is a good idea to use the instruments or muscle-test *before* the actual session. It is an especially good idea for new clients for whom these energetic techniques might appear quite strange. When a client is comfortable with the instruments, we begin the session.

I asked Jim, while we were both tapping slowly on the side of our hands and also watching the bio-tensor, if the cause of his present vision problem was from this life or a past life. The indication of the bio-tensor was a past life but he was disappointed because he wanted to clear the event of himself as a nine-year-old child in this lifetime.

I began by first doing a few rounds of regular EFT on his disappointment at not going right away to meet with his nine-year-old self. Once he was relaxed and even laughing a little about being impatient, we continued.

I asked him to continue tapping gently and slowly on the side of his hand and, with his eyes closed, to take some relaxing breaths and then to fill himself with a light and that light would help his subconscious see whatever it needed to remember. I asked him to give the light a color. He said it was pale yellow.

I asked his pale yellow subconscious to take us to where we needed to be to clear the problem in his vision of not being able to maintain the focus of his eyes.

While he was doing this, I tapped gently and slower than usual, on his points. I also spoke very quietly and slowly. Every so often, while I was tapping, I repeated that we were allowing his pale yellow subconscious to take us where we need to be. As I often do in this work, I also reminded him several times, always speaking softly and slowly, sometimes whispering, that he is completely safe here with me.

I asked the basic questions while holding the bio-tensor, sometimes moving it near his eyes, sometimes moving it near his hands or his heart. I asked the pale yellow light to show us if in the lifetime that we are looking for, was he a man? a woman? a child? a baby?

The indication of the bio-tensor was a child. I asked him if that felt right to him and he immediately said, *"a little girl"*. The bio-tensor was reacting so strongly that I stopped using it so it would not break. Something important was happening and I no longer felt the need to use the instrument.

I am learning a lot about different approaches to use from the psychiatrist Dr. Brian Weiss. As mentioned earlier, Dr.

Weiss has taken thousands of people back to their past lives through past life regression for the purpose of healing. He uses a light form of hypnotism. Instead, I use EFT. If you are skilled in both, you could certainly combine the two methods.

I sometimes ask clients questions that I learned from studying the work of Dr. Weiss. For example, once clients have located another lifetime, I might ask them to look down at their feet to see what kind of shoes, if any, they are wearing. With the answer, we can gain more information about the circumstances of the past life. In this session with Jim, I asked that question. He was quiet for a while as I continued a light and slow tapping on his acupoints. After a few minutes, he answered that the little girl was barefoot.

I asked him to tell me about the place where the little girl was. Jim described "a rocky, sandy place".

I asked him if he was looking at the place through the eyes of the little girl or was he looking at the little girl. He said "both". Usually, in my experience, clients are either revisiting the event as the person they were in their past life, or they are revisiting it while looking at themselves in the other life. Either can have highly fruitful results.

I asked him if he knew the date or the country. He did not.

In following a brilliant method used by Dr. Weiss to learn more about the event, I asked him to look around and see if anyone else was there. The purpose of looking for other people is to ask them questions such as where they are or what the date is.

He said that no one else was there.

I asked Jim to have the little girl without shoes continue looking around this rocky, sandy place so maybe she could find someone to ask where they were and what the date was. I continued to tap lightly.

Please note that I use the words of the client when I ask questions or discuss the event. This is always important when doing either this lifetime or previous lifetime EFT.

Finally, he said that an old man carrying a shovel was there, walking away from the little girl, who was my client in another life. Jim was confused for a moment, watching the old man walk away, then the old man with the shovel disappeared and Jim said that he immediately saw his nine-year-old self clearly this lifetime.

We were able to clear the event when Jim was nine in a standard EFT session. The troublesome event was his mother's death and it was a beautiful tapping session that greatly improved his ability to focus his vision.

So, what happened in that session? I believe we needed to first contact that past life event as the little girl with the man and the shovel to unblock the event from this life when Jim was nine years old. We just touched on the past life, while tapping, and that was enough to clear the way for his nine-year-old little boy to be seen and for the boy to finally find peace and closure in the passing of his mother. The event, when he was nine, was a moment in his present life that he did not want to see.

*As long as you are not aware of the continual
law of 'Die and Be Born Again' you are
merely a vague guest on a dark Earth.*

JOHANN WOLFGANG VON GOETHE

*When You Share Past Life
Experiences with Others*

The expression, "It's a small world", became more than a cliché for me during two EFT sessions in which I also found myself involved in my clients' past life traumas.

The first time it happened, I was working with an EFT client who I'll call Bob. He was in his mid-twenties and had been experiencing terrible headaches for several years. The headaches were becoming more frequent and more painful. Because I am not a doctor, I always emphasize, with my clients who ask for my help with EFT for severe physical problems, that they need to first speak with a physician. I want to be absolutely certain that the causes of their complaints are not physical in nature. Bob, in fact, had previously undergone several medical tests that did not show a physical reason for his pain.

I asked him to keep a journal before our first session, noting everything he ate and drank as well as noting the weather conditions or any obvious stressful situations, to see if he could find a clear cause of the headaches.

During the initial interview with Bob, he told me that the first time he remembered having a headache he was on vacation on an island in the Caribbean. It was a "dream vacation" for him with fellow university students. During our first two EFT sessions, we were able to clear some troublesome issues connected with the headaches but his pain continued. At our third session I asked if we could explore the possibility of a past life connection to the headaches.

His expression of surprise at my question was one I will always remember. He laughed a little and then he said that he was willing to try anything. In previous sessions we were able to successfully use kinesiology and because Bob is a rather conservative young man, I had not yet used the bio-tensor or pendulum in working with him.

If you use kinesiology (muscle-testing) with yourself or another person, you might find that it does not work. The responses you get from the test questions might not be correct. If I say, "my name is Judy" my arm should be rigid for me because that is really my name. If my arm goes weak on slight pressure, the muscle-test is not working. In that case, there are the alternatives of the pendulum or the bio-tensor to try.

In my experience, these methods might fail to work if the "tester" does not trust them or has pre-conceived opinions about the answers to his or her questions or if the person being tested does not drink enough water and is dehydrated or eats an excessive amount of white sugar. My theory about the sugar is that it destroys minerals in the body and we need balanced minerals for the energy to flow in the body and give us accurate responses during energetic testing. As I am not a scientist or doctor, I offer this theory just between you and me.

Once a past life incident has been located, I prefer to not use kinesiology simply because the physical contact might interrupt the highly relaxed state that we need in past life work.

For that reason, the bio-tensor or pendulum are, for me, the best "assistants" to use during sessions. At the time of Bob's session, I did not yet have a bio-tensor and I was hoping that the pendulum might not seem too strange or offensive for him.

For those reasons, I introduced Bob to the pendulum before we actually began the session. I asked him many questions using the pendulum which I held over the open palm of one of his hands. He could clearly see that the responses of the pendulum corresponded to his feelings. He could even, without using words, but by only thinking of answers to my questions, note the correct movement of the pendulum.

A few times he tried to trick the pendulum by saying, for example, "My dog's name is Cookie" but the pendulum did not move at all. When he confessed that he did not even have a dog and that explained the lack of movement, he had gained trust in my use of the pendulum!

Bob's intention for the session was only to eliminate the pain and be normal. He said that he did not care about knowing the cause unless knowing the cause got rid of the pain.

We began the session in the standard way. I tapped lightly on the side of his hand (the Karate Chop Point), while he repeated the EFT Set-up phrase three times:

"Even though I sometimes get terrible burning pain headaches, I accept myself anyway.

Even though it's true that I sometimes get terrible headache pain, I really do accept myself completely.

Even though I sometimes get terrible burning pain headaches, I accept myself totally, I really mean it, and I choose, with all my heart, to have a happy and normal head."

I tapped slowly and softly while asking him to repeat reminder statements such as:

"I sometimes get terrible burning headache pain…"

After a couple of rounds of tapping on various reminder phrases concerned with the headaches, I asked Bob to take some nice deep breaths. I told him that I wanted to ask his subconscious for some information and that he did not need to answer my questions with words. I asked him to imagine a light and to give it the color of his choice. His subconscious would use that light to lead us back into time to find the beginning of his headaches so they could be eliminated. He chose the color light blue for the light. I also lightly squeezed his thumbs and fingertips. As mentioned earlier, I often use this method to help clients relax.

> Remember that relaxation is a key to success in past life work.

I slowly and continuously tapped while gently reminding him, every so often, to keep on looking for the beginning of his headache pain. I spoke softly and slowly repeatedly asking him for the first time in his entire existence that he felt the same headache pain. He clearly remembered his experience on the Caribbean island. I asked him to bring that light blue light to the island and asked his subconscious to lead us to a time before his visit to the Caribbean, when the pain began.

I reminded Bob to breathe gently. Sometimes, when people are looking into their distant past for the first time, it is natural to become tense. For this reason it is important to guide clients to have a relaxed in and out breath.

During this tapping, I also asked him to imagine the blue light under him, holding him up in the air now, like a cloud. The reason I added this was because I felt that it was not easy for Bob to relax. The feeling that a cloud is holding us up in the air, while doing focused breathing, can be relaxing. Try it for yourself sometime.

Soon after that, he said that he smelled something burning. I assured him that everything was fine, nothing here was burning and to follow that smell with the light from his subconscious to find out what it is. His breathing became faster and he started to talk about smoke, a lot of smoke.

He said, almost as if he could not believe it, that he feels like he is on a big old Spanish warship with many sails and it is on fire. He described everything in great detail. He said that pieces of wood were falling all around him and there were so many loud noises, people were screaming and there was no escape.

His eyes were tearing and so were mine. Often, doing this work, practitioners feel trauma along with our clients. In our training we learn important methods of protecting ourselves from these sympathetic problems. This for me was different in that I knew without a doubt that I had also been on that Spanish galleon in another lifetime with the man who Bob had been in his other life. I heard the explosions that he talked about. I felt the heat of the fire. I felt that there was no escape.

I checked my feelings with the pendulum and its movements confirmed all of my personal feelings about my presence on that ship. I knew I could tap on myself after this session and my first responsibility was to my client. I asked him to repeat my words while I continued tapping about different aspects of his experience:

It's possible that I am on the burning ship, that's how it feels...the big Spanish warship. It's on fire. It's terrible. Smoke is everywhere. Things are falling on me. I can't escape. People are screaming. I can't believe what I see...But it's real...My face is burning......"

While tapping on Bob, I gradually moved this experience into the past tense with Reminder Phrases such as:

"The ship was on fire...It was a long time ago...It was terrible...It happened then...I can't change the burning ship... It's part of my history...I can learn from it...It's over...I'm here now...Safe...In Italy..."

After four or five rounds of tapping Bob opened his eyes. We both drank a lot of water. He talked a lot, saying things like, "So, it's really true! That was me! I was there on that ship! I know it was real! This is amazing! I never thought about living before now! I think I feel different but I don't know how I feel! I feel good but I'm confused. I'm so lucky to be here and alive now."

When we ended that session, I asked Bob to contact me if he had another headache. I telephoned him twice but he reported that he was fine. I have not heard from him again. That session was three years ago.

The only other time I have been in a past life trauma with a client was about a year ago. This event was, coincidently, also at sea.

My client was a woman in her sixties. She had become accustomed to revisiting her past lives in working with me. She had been extremely ill for most of her life. Thanks to EFT she was making a good recovery. In this particular session, she remembered being a female Japanese pearl diver.

In the middle of the session with her, I began to feel terrible. I felt physical pains. I even began to cry. The client had her eyes closed and was so much involved in her past life event that she did not know I was crying. As she continued to tell me the story of her event, even with her eyes closed, she began to apologize profusely for killing me in that lifetime.

If in working with the past lives of another person, you happen to find yourself involved in the same trauma, I have some suggestions:

I recommend following the advice given to the little fish "Nemo" in the movie of the same name. Nemo was told to "just keep swimming" but in our case, "just keep tapping"! Tap on the event to whatever degree you can enter it when the client is there with you. In other words, do not stop the process simply because you feel included in a client's traumatic past life experience. In order to do my best for the client during the session, I consciously focused on keeping myself in the present moment, while continuing to do the work by feeling my feet on the floor, my derrière on the chair and my attention totally on the client who was sitting on the chair in front of me. If you find yourself, in another lifetime, in a client's past event, you'll want to also tap on yourself, for yourself, as soon as the session is finished.

> *Friends are all souls that we've known in other lives. We're drawn to each other. Even if I have only known them a day, it doesn't matter.*
>
> GEORGE HARRISON

Automatically Arriving at a Past Life Memory

When working with a client on an event of this lifetime and he or she says something that is obviously connected with an experience that could not possibly have happened in this life, it is important to follow the client in whatever he or she is saying. This is a classic example of an Automatic Client, Category 3 in Chapter 5.

This was a Skype EFT session with, Bertha, a 45-year-old woman. She lives in the United Kingdom. She was suffering from chest pains for which doctors had found no physical cause. We had been working for a while on a traumatic event she had when she was in high school in this lifetime when she suddenly said *"...they look just like Roman gladiators...they were Roman gladiators..."*

It would have been a mistake if I would have said something like, "No, no! We're not talking about gladiators. Stay focused on high school." Instead, I said, *"Well, okay. Keep your eyes closed and tell me more about the Roman gladiators..."*

Many EFT practitioners work very comfortably with clients using either the telephone or by Skype via the Internet. I rarely use the telephone simply because I live in an area of mountains and hills in Northern Italy where telephone connections are not always reliable. Instead, Skype works well most of the time using my computer and the computer of the client. My Skype clients live all over the world. The main requirement is that both computers, at whatever distance, have high speed Internet connections.

With past life EFT sessions via Skype, my clients and I have the great advantage of being able to see each other during sessions. I usually teach clients to muscle-test themselves as well as use a pendulum. I usually ask Skype clients to use these methods so they can check their responses while we are working.

With this particular session, Bertha tapped on the event with the gladiators, finding herself as one of them. I did not want to interrupt the progress she was making by asking her to check the event with muscle-testing or her pendulum, so I worked with her until the event was less intense.

When she felt that the intensity, which began with a high SUD number (please refer to Chapter 9), was reduced to an intensity of 2 on a 0 to 10 scale, I asked her to check the traumatic event in this way using her pendulum:

"Even though I felt that pain in my chest as a Roman gladiator, (the pendulum was spinning very quickly and in

a wide confirming clock-wise circle as she said those words) *I now feel better and I understand what happened to me as a gladiator and my chest feels fine. Absolutely fine."*

❧

When we returned to the traumatic event of this lifetime, in high school, it had no intensity at all, her chest felt, in her words, "finally relaxed" and she was very happy

> *I did not begin when I was born, nor when I was conceived. I have been growing, developing, through incalculable myriads of millenniums. All my previous selves have their voices, echoes, promptings in me. Oh, incalculable times again shall I be born.*
>
> JACK LONDON

❧

Finding the Cause of Marie's Hearing Problems

A young woman from France was staying at *Cascina Rosso* for a week's vacation with her family. I'll call her Marie. I speak a little French and she spoke a little English, enough so we could communicate with each other just a little.

I noticed that she wore hearing aids in both of her ears and so I asked her what the problem was. She told me that a few years ago, she gradually began to lose her hearing. She saw a few specialists who advised surgery to replace the insides of her ears. The cost would have been about 10,000 Euros (about $13,000) for each ear, without any guarantee of success. We tried EFT.

We worked with EFT on the events of the same day that she began to lose her hearing. There had been a serious emotional trauma that day. As part of that trauma, things were said that she did not want to hear. Once we cleared that trauma I was, of course, hoping that she would have some improvement in her hearing. Instead, nothing changed.

Marie was very interested in exploring the idea of past lives. She was a Category 1, Believer Client as defined in Chapter 5. She removed one of her hearing aids because she said she could hear me reasonably well by only using one of them.

We began the session in the usual way: I asked about her intention for the session and she was very certain that she wanted to regain her hearing. I explained about the bio-tensor and asked her to take some relaxing breaths and to try to clear her mind of outside thoughts as she focused on her breathing. I asked her to imagine a big, soft cloud under her, holding her up in the air. I asked her to choose a color for the cloud and she chose pink.

I tapped softly and slowly on the side of her hand and then gently squeezed her fingertips while speaking very quietly to her. I told her that I would be talking to and asking questions of her subconscious and she did not need to speak. I asked her subconscious if it was okay for me to ask some questions for the purpose of helping Marie hear better.

The bio-tensor indicated a "no" response. I asked another question of Marie's subconscious: *Are you protecting Marie by not wanting her to hear?* The response of the bio-tensor was "yes".

EFT practitioners often work with a category of problems known as *secondary benefits*. These secondary benefits occur when the subconscious finds it in some way beneficial to have and/or keep a problem.

We did EFT: *"Even though your subconscious wants to protect you and does not want to answer my questions, you can accept and love all of you, including your subconscious. It's true that your subconscious wants to protect you, that's its job and that's wonderful and I also want to help your subconscious protect you. We are all on the same side, you me and your subconscious..."*

With that, Marie laughed a little and I asked again to her subconscious if I could ask some questions for the purpose of helping Marie. This time, the response of the bio-tensor was "yes". Whenever it is appropriate in either this lifetime or past life work, the use of humor can bring welcomed benefits.

After asking the basic questions, Marie's subconscious took us to another lifetime where she was a four-year-old little girl in Spain. Marie told me that she clearly saw herself as this little girl, in her parents' bedroom, standing at the foot of their bed. Her mother was standing next to her, crying and her father, who she adored, was lying in the bed.

I used one of my favorite EFT techniques called "Matrix Reimprinting" (see Resource Section) as I took Marie back to another life when she was the little girl in Spain.

I encourage anyone interested in learning EFT or expanding their EFT skills to also learn Matrix Reimprinting.

In this session, we learned that the little girl loved her father but he had died and was lying in his bed until he would be taken away for the funeral. Her mother was also in the bedroom. The little girl wanted to get into the bed to play and cuddle with her daddy, not understanding that he was dead. The mother was devastated by her husband's death and about trying to hold her daughter away from him and she hit the little girl with both fists, hard on her ears. While the mother kept on screaming at the little girl, the child was happy to not hear her mother screaming at her anymore; everything became silent for the little girl.

After that session, Marie continued to only use one hearing aid because there was a small improvement in her hearing. After a few days, her hearing was bad again and there was obviously more work to do. Her vacation ended and she returned to France. I have referred her to one of my advanced EFT students who is fluent in the French language. They are working together on Skype looking for additional Past Life Trauma Sequence (PLTS) elements in Marie's other lifetimes and happily making progress.

I know I am deathless. No doubt I have died myself ten thousand times before.

WALT WHITMAN

Paying Attention to Clues

As noted in Category 4 of Chapter 5, practitioners need to be very alert to specific body movements or words that clients use during sessions. The expressions of Clue-Giver Clients can be *signals* that we need to follow in finding our way to the key negative events of this or previous lifetimes.

I had been treating a male client with severe long term sinus problems that sometimes made it hard to breathe or to do his work as a school teacher. EFT was helping him to reduce the number of sinus attacks but his problem continued. I worked with this teacher in the days before I was doing much work with past lives so I did not consider suggesting that approach to resolving his sinus problem.

In the session that I want to tell you about, he had arrived with very bad sinuses. During the session, he continued, over and over again, to emotionally complain about the agony of the bridge of his nose saying things like, *"Oh, this bridge... this bridge...why me...this is too bad...this bridge...I can't go on...I hate it...you don't understand how I hate it...no one understands..."* While he was complaining, I was tapping on his acupoints and I asked his subconscious to look for a bridge, any bridge.

After some time passed, while I continued to tap, he began talking about a bridge. It was hard to understand everything he said because he was enormously emotional and his sinuses were badly blocked. I continued tapping and I asked him to tell me about the bridge.

He was describing something. I could not understand all the details. His description was during a war. There were bodies and debris and thick water below him and terrible smells. He was crawling on a broken bridge. He was unbelievably upset about the terrible smells of bodies and objects below him.

I tapped many rounds on anything and everything I heard him say. As discussed earlier, it is important to use the client's words when tapping. I did thirty rounds with him, maybe more. I tapped mostly on all the bad things about that bridge. When we finally cleared that horrible event of another lifetime, he was exhausted. He blew his nose over and over again and that session, years ago, was finally the end of his sinus problems!

So as through a glass and darkly, the age long strife I see,
Where I fought in many guises, many names, but always me.

GENERAL GEORGE S. PATTON

Children and Their Past Lives

Children are usually easy to work with, they love tapping and their results are quite rapid. Even though I have enjoyed working with many children with EFT, at this writing, I have had the opportunity of working only a few times with the past lives of children. There are many others, including medical doctors and child psychiatrists, who have documented what appear to be the remembered past lives of thousands of children. (Please refer to the Resource Section)

When approaching the idea of working with a child's past life, I do not call it a *past life*; I only refer to it as *pretending*.

Eddie is a happy and bright eight year old. I had worked with him for various problems and I also taught him how to tap on himself. He is used to tapping when problems come up between him and his two sisters, his parents, friends or teachers. Until recently, he was a good student and always enthusiastic about going to school and doing homework.

His mother called to tell me that he had a new teacher and that he hated her. He was doing badly in school and refused to do his homework. When he arrived for an EFT session, he looked terrible. He had lost weight and looked sad.

In our previous sessions, I always used the crystal pendulum because he loved it. He called it "Judy's magic pendulum". I asked him some questions in order to find out, in his own words, what we needed to work on, if anything. He did not have his typical enthusiasm. He mostly just shrugged his shoulders at my questions such as, "How are you doing? How is the family? How's school? Are you playing soccer?"

Finally he said, with his face all twisted, "I hate my teacher! I really hate her! And she hates me!" I asked him if he was ready to do some tapping. *"Sure"* he said, *"but I'll still hate her. Hold up your magic pendulum and you'll see how much I hate her".*

I held the pendulum over one of Eddie's open palms. The pendulum spun almost out of control while he was telling me how much he hated the teacher and how much she hated him.

I asked him if this was a good day for pretending and we checked it with the pendulum. The response was positive. Then I asked if it was a good day for really, really pretending. The pendulum again responded positively. Eddie loves to pretend and has a great imagination so he was gradually looking a little more enthusiastic.

Eddie closed his eyes to start the session. He was tapping on the side of his hand and then I tapped on some of his acupoints. I rarely tap all the acupoints with children because they often require less tapping. I asked him to think about the teacher, to remember something he didn't like that happened when he was with her.

> *"Remember a bad thing that happened when you were with her."*

Then I asked him to pretend that another person, maybe another boy or a girl or a grown-up man or a grown-up woman is also having a big problem like he had with the teacher. I asked him to just imagine it, to really pretend.

The pendulum was not moving at all. I told Eddie that I was watching the pendulum and it was not moving. I explained to him that it meant he was not really focusing on pretending about another person having a problem like his problem with the teacher. I asked him to pretend even more. Soon the pendulum began to respond.

He spoke very little and so while I continued to tap, I slowly and quietly repeated anything I heard him say. For the most part, I said encouraging words like, *That's right...good...yes...very good...*

I continued tapping EFT rounds for maybe 10 minutes. Then, Eddie opened his eyes. He jumped up on the chair he was sitting on. He pretended to strangle himself, ran around, acting out an imaginary fight. He took an imaginary sword from his side, was making lots of noises, yelling, and then he fell on the floor and cried.

All the time he was running around in the room, screaming and yelling and having an imaginary battle, I did surrogate EFT tapping on myself for him to help him get through whatever bad moments he was revisiting. [14]

---

[14]   Judith Rivera Rosso, *EFT & Life* e-Book

While he was still lying on my floor, I sat down next to him and gently tapped and touched some of his acupoints and said things like, *That was so hard, no one knows how hard it was, but you know. It was a long time ago, it's okay now, you're safe, you can be happy, I'm so proud of you. You are so smart.* I "tapped-in" many positive statements. Then we had some juice and cookies and his mom arrived to take him home.

In a few days Eddie's mom called to ask, "What did you do? Eddie is doing his homework, he likes school again and he doesn't even complain about that teacher at all!"

I do not know the details about what happened in Eddie's memory or the details of what was happening during the imaginary battle that took place during our session. I also do not know why he cried. I do know that during Eddie's eight years in this lifetime as Eddie, there had not been any fierce sword battles such as the one that took place during the session. I do believe that whatever happened, Eddie was revisiting some event while tapping and receiving surrogate tapping. Whatever happened, it was good that he cleared the event.

From the perspective of a child subject...
the memories that he experiences of a former life
seem just as real – just as much true memories –as
memories he may have of events since he was born.

IAN STEVENSON, MD
CHILD PSYCHIATRIST

Eating Problems

Please note: You might find that the details of the following session are too challenging for you; if you feel you have a "weak stomach", I suggest that you skip it. If, however, you work as a professional in the healing arts, I suggest that you read it for the information it contains and you might also want to tap on yourself as you do. JRR

Here is an example of a client with severe eating problems with which she had suffered for her entire life. My client, a woman I'll call Evelyn, is in her early 70's. We had been working on her problems for several months, making progress in many areas of her life, but she was still unable to digest most food and generally uninterested in eating; she looked emaciated.

She was scheduled for a session with me on the same day that there was a medical doctor from Germany staying with my husband and I at our Agriturismo, *Cascina Rosso*. I asked the doctor if he would meet with this client and give me his opinion, a kind of consultation while on holiday.

At the start of the session, he tried to muscle-test her, looking for the reason for her eating problems. He pushed gently on her arm but she was too frail, thin and weak to support even the gentlest pressure on her arm. So, I held one of her hands in my hand and he did surrogate muscle-testing on me for her, asking her to date the lifetime that began her present eating problem.

His questions were:

"Was it in this lifetime?"
"No"
"Last lifetime?"
"No"

And so he continued until my arm held firm against his pressure at *eleven lifetimes ago.*

In my next EFT session with Evelyn, I used the bio-tensor to help check our direction while I asked questions and gently tapped and touched her points. We learned that eleven lifetimes ago she was a little boy, alone and trapped in a cave that he could not leave. The little boy in the cave was surrounded by worms. She, the client, remembering this distant event, was screaming and crying during this session and I continued to tap. Evelyn felt the worms on her even now and, while I was tapping on her, she tried to push them away from her.

As EFT practitioners we do our best to lead our clients as gently as possible to key past events that need to be cleared. Gary Craig has even created an EFT technique called "The Tearless Trauma Technique" for that purpose. In the days before EFT, psychologists and psychiatrists often inadvertently re-traumatized their clients by having them repeatedly "re-live" past traumas. This is not the case with EFT. The tapping effect along the meridians of the Energy System while re-visiting a past trauma can do wonders in clearing the stresses and *zzztts* of the trauma. This often results in the emotional freedom that can bring the healing for which EFT is so well known.

In Evelyn's case, however, I felt that my client's strong upset while I was tapping on her could be the breakthrough that would finally bring peace and healing into her life. My instincts paid off and in just a few minutes she was calm.

I asked questions and we discovered that those worms, at first, had been the little boy's friends. They jumped around and danced for him and they made him laugh.

He loved the worms, his friends, in the beginning of the event and then he got hungry because there was no food and he was alone with the worms. The little boy began to eat them and afterwards he got sick. When we tapped on different aspects of him eating his "friends", that's when we began to make real progress.

While I did many rounds of continuous tapping on Evelyn, she repeated my words in which she asked the worms to forgive her for eating them. We continued tapping on beginning to understand why she ate them because there was no other food. And finally, we did many rounds of tapping on her forgiving herself for eating her little friends. That was the real breakthrough when she forgave herself.

This, one of my most challenging clients, began to make real progress after that session for an event of eleven lifetimes ago. Eating the worms was only one aspect of that event and we have been able to return to it very easily by relaxing and returning to a part of the event about which we already had some information from the previous session.

Our consciousness survives physical death.

DEEPAK CHOPRA, MD

Additional Sessions with Evelyn

Using a bio-tensor, pendulum or muscle-testing can be a great help in quickly finding other aspects of past events. Some questions that I use to find those aspects are: *In that cave, eleven lifetimes ago, did you _hear_ anything that we need to clear?*

I like to ask about the physical senses: *Did you _see_ or _smell_ or _touch_ anything else in that cave that we need to clear away to help you eat food more easily now?*

Sometimes, we accumulate either obvious or subtle habits that have powerful and lasting effects on our well-being and us. Eleven lifetimes with a negative habit is a long time! The traumas of the past can also create, consciously or subconsciously within us, limiting beliefs that we might be carrying around with us in our Energy System through lifetimes as demonstrated by the Past Life Trauma Sequence.

When these destructive negative habits or limiting beliefs are cleared away, we often need help to notice that they, as well as all the accumulations of negative energy attached to them, are also gone.

This idea is similar to the *cognitive shift* idea of standard EFT in which clients do not always realize that they are free from a negative habit until a practitioner indicates the shift to them. In this case, the instrument of the bio-tensor or pendulum and the use of muscle-testing are beautiful things to help a client notice when they have become free from a negative habit or limiting belief.

Evelyn has begun eating a healthy diet and she actually enjoys eating now. She is happy to be gaining some needed weight.

Hallucinations or Memories?

Please remember that I am not a medical professional and that I am neither anti-medicine nor anti-psychiatry. I do believe, however, that if Evelyn had found her way to a traditional psychiatrist instead of, as she did, to me for help with EFT, she would possibly have been confined to a mental asylum. Once confined, she would possibly have been drugged with pharmaceuticals and caught up in a dwindling spiral of medication and incarceration; I shudder to think of what her life might have become.

I also believe that she might have been psychiatrically diagnosed as having "hallucinations". She reported "seeing and hearing" scenes that had no connection with her present experiences, people or places with which she was familiar. She referred to the scenes as "flashes". The flashes appeared without warning and sometimes included terrifying events that drove her into fear, panic and/or anger.

I sometimes used a technique for troublesome events by asking her to draw the flashes and we treated them with EFT. In spite of trying a variety of fabulous EFT techniques, she rarely found relief, which means that the intensity of her flashes rarely became zero.

Many people report having unexplained flashes from time to time but, for some reason, Evelyn's flashes seemed to pile up on her and she would sometimes experience an accumulation of frightening events in one single flash.

I am happy to report that Evelyn is almost completely "flash-free" as a result of treating her flashes as past life memories with EFT. In addition, as she was healing from those memories and becoming free from them with tapping, I encouraged her, through using life-coaching EFT for her present life to help her find and develop her life purpose. It turned out that Evelyn is actually a highly creative lady who finally has the emotional freedom within her to express her creative talents.

I can only wonder how many people have been diagnosed with delusions and are wasting-away in asylums because of what appear to be hallucinations but might instead be memories from distant times and places.

Today (2008), people who believe in reincarnation
may outnumber those who do not.

JIM B. TUCKER, MD
CHILD PSYCHIATRIST

Chapter 8

DO-IT-YOURSELF PAST LIFE HEALING

One morning, I woke up with a sharp, burning pain in my back. Before discovering EFT, I had spent many years suffering from severe back pain (as well as other problems that are gone thanks to EFT). On that particular morning of waking in pain, the first thing I wanted to do was to get my bio-tensor.

I managed to painfully find my way to the bio-tensor. I asked if I needed to go to the hospital. The indication was negative. I tapped on myself the best I could, in spite of the intense pain. I tapped for the pain until it was slightly reduced and I could begin to think a little more clearly.

My intention was for my back to feel fine. I also wanted to know what happened to me so that I did not let it happen again! I asked many questions using the bio-tensor. I don't remember all of the questions but here are two of them just in case you find yourself in a similar situation.

Is there any physical reason for this pain?
Did I have an injury in these days that I don't
remember?

The responses of the bio-tensor were negative
The response was positive when I asked:

Can I know the reason for this pain?

I tapped on:

Even though I don't know the reason for this pain, I
am willing to know why my back hurts and I am asking my
subconscious to let me know what happened to my back...

I did my best to relax, breathing slowly in and out. I focused on my breathing. I imagined a big white cloud under me and holding me in the air. I remember that I began thinking about the day before. I was having a haircut. There was a woman waiting for her turn. I watched the lady's reflection in the mirror. She was looking at me for a long time. I remember thinking that she looked unhappy, angry and kind of mean.

As I tapped on myself I also began to remember that during the night I had a dream about being alone in the woods and a young American Indian man shot me with a huge silver arrow in the back of my leg. The arrow hit my leg and then fell on the ground, making a loud metallic sound. The sound woke me up. And when I woke up, I was in severe back pain.

I checked with the bio-tensor to see if there was any connection between the dream and the lady in the salon. The movement was positive. I asked another question using the bio-tensor:

Was that angry and unhappy woman in the salon yesterday, the one who kept looking at me, the same Indian man I saw in my dream last night?

The response of the bio-tensor was negative. So I asked a different question. I continued to use the bio-tensor but by now I was so connected to these memories that my intuition already knew the answers:

> *Did we know each other in another life as Indians?*
> *Did we hurt each other?*

The bio-tensor confirmed what I already felt intuitively. I did standard EFT to clear the trauma of the specific event of our distant American Indian past. By lunchtime I was perfectly fine and, once again, totally grateful to EFT.

What happened? Could I have prevented the back pain I had when the lady in the salon re-entered my life? Yes, I believe I could have. Based on the many experiences I have had as an EFT practitioner as well as my own personal experiences with EFT, I believe that when I was in the salon I slipped out of the present moment and did not notice it.

That painful experience was, for me and hopefully also for you, a reminder about the importance of living in the present moment. It was also a reminder about the importance of staying alert when, because of any circumstance, we notice that we have slipped out of the present.

That is the moment to do something about it so that we can maintain our healthy and happy state of life!

When those potentially destructive moments arrive, we have many choices about actions we can take to bring ourselves back into the present. Those actions can be as simple as focusing on our breathing, feeling our feet on the floor, looking around for those things we are grateful for that make us feel good.

We can also tap on our EFT "finger points" (see Chapter 9) even with our hands in our pockets so no one knows we are tapping in public! We can give ourselves a full EFT session. If we are not able to resolve the problem ourselves, we can find an EFT Practitioner to help us.

Believing as I do in the theory of reincarnation, I live in the hope that if not in this birth, in some other birth I shall be able to hug all of humanity in friendly embrace.

MAHATMA GANDHI

Chapter 9

HOW TO DO EFT TAPPING

The cause of all negative emotions
is a disruption in the body's energy system.

GARY CRAIG

Before writing *The Great Joy of Healing Past Lives,* I wrote two EFT books. *EFT & Life* is available as an e-book through the Internet and contains both basic and advanced information. You can easily download it by going to my site: www.eftitalia.com and clicking on the English language tab *The EFT & Life* e-book.

The other is a published book, *EFT & Vita,* in the Italian language. Information about both of these books is available on various Internet sites as well as www.eftitalia.com.

I have borrowed some of the illustrations and tapping information that you will find in this chapter from my previously published books.

Tapping is done with the tips of your fingers, usually the index and middle finger together. In some situations, you will use several fingertips at the same time. You simply tap lightly, about 5 to 10 times, sometimes more, on specific tapping points of The Energy System. The client is fully clothed during EFT sessions.

1. At the same time that specific acupoints are lightly tapped…
2. …the person is focused on the actual problem or specific memories that are connected with the problem that the person wants to resolve.

The Intensity of the Problem

At the start of every EFT session with other people or yourself, you want to establish something called the SUD intensity. A SUD stands for Subjective Unit of Discomfort. It is an excellent way to measure the intensity of the problem at the start as well as at times during the session. It is an easy measurement to make.

You simply ask the client to imagine a scale with numbers on it that go from zero to ten. Zero represents no problem at all. Instead, the number ten on the scale would represent the maximum discomfort, fear, anxiety, pain, etc. that the client is feeling. There are, of course, the other numbers of intensity between 0 and 10.

It is a good idea to write down the SUD number at the start of the session. You will be able to compare it to the SUD number when the session is completed to measure your progress and give an indication of further work to do. It is also helpful to check with the client on the level of intensity during the session.

The Setup

The Setup is required in starting every EFT session. Its function is to correct the polarity of our energy system. If the polarity of the energy system is not correct, the steps of EFT will not work.

It is a simple and quick procedure that corrects the situation of reversed energetic polarity called "psychological reversal".

Psychological Reversal

Psychological reversal is not present with everyone all the time. Gary Craig explains it in The EFT Manual by comparing the way the energy system functions in our bodies to the way batteries work in a tape recorder. If the batteries are put into the recorder incorrectly or reversed, the tape recorder simply does not work because the energy does not flow correctly.

> I have certainly had days when I felt as though my own "batteries" were reversed! We do not, however, always feel our psychological reversal because it is working on us subconsciously. **Our negative thinking is the biggest cause of reversed energetic polarity referred to in EFT as psychological reversal.** Please refer to *The EFT Manual* for a detailed discussion of this very important subject.

Where exactly are those tapping points?

Basic EFT is easy to learn. Once you memorize the *tapping points*, also known as *points* or *acupoints*, they will be yours forever. As you tap, follow the location of the tapping points that you see on the drawings that follow. When Gary Craig wrote *The EFT Manual*, tapping was done on one side of the body. Since those early days of EFT, he has been teaching the EFT community that good results are often had by tapping on both sides of the body at the same time. You can, therefore, tap on one or both sides of the body at the same time. You can use the right hand to tap the points along the left side of the body or vice-versa.

The Basic Tapping Points of EFT

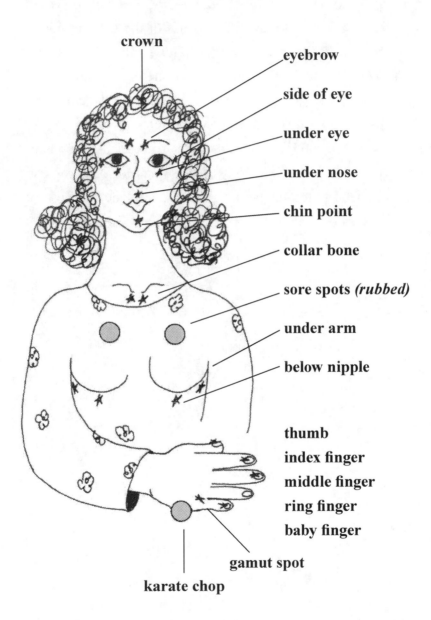

crown

eyebrow

side of eye

under eye

under nose

chin point

collar bone

sore spots *(rubbed)*

under arm

below nipple

thumb
index finger
middle finger
ring finger
baby finger

gamut spot

karate chop

The Karate Chop Point

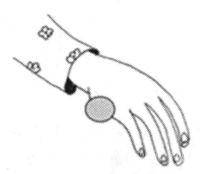

Tap with the fingers of one hand, on the Karate Chop Point of the other hand.

This point is located on the outside fleshy part of the side of the hand, between the baby finger and the wrist.

The Setup, continued

Instead of tapping on the side of the hand, you can rub one or both of the Sore Spots. Refer to the previous drawing, "The Basic Tapping Points of EFT" to locate the Sore Spots.

The Sore Spots are tender areas located on the chest.
They are about 4 centimeters (2 inches) in diameter.

When doing The Setup, either tap on the Karate Chop point or rub the Sore Spots in a circular motion with the fingertips. Rub in either direction. Do not tap the Sore Spots.

These spots are in the areas of lymphatic drainage and they are sore when there is congestion. People have these spots in slightly different places on the chest. You will know when you find the correct location of the Sore Spots because they feel a little sore or tender when you rub them.

As with the Karate Chop points at the sides of your hands, there is a connection on this area of the chest with the polarity of the energy system.

It is best to rub both Sore Spots at the same time. If they are very painful, tap, instead, on the Karate Chop point. You might only be able to rub one Sore Spot instead of two—perhaps you and your client are working on the telephone, using one hand to hold the telephone receiver. If rubbing only one Sore Spot, always choose the left one. The reason, according to EFT expert, Sandra Randomski, ND is that there are 70 percent more glands of the lymphatic drainage system on the left side of the chest.

The Setup Affirmation

While you either tap on the Karate Chop point or rub the Sore Spots, repeat an affirmation three times. This Setup affirmation has two basic parts with two basic functions:

1) it states the problem in a word or a few words and
2) it creates self-acceptance in spite of having the problem.

There are many variations to the self-acceptance part of the Setup which might include, for example self-love, forgiveness, respect and/or understanding.

An excellent explanation of why it is important to use various wordings of *self-acceptance* when tapping can be found in a free video by Dr. Dawson Church. The video, entitled "Neural Bundles", lasts about 7 minutes. To view it, simply go to the site, www.eftuniverse.com, click "videos" then click "Neural Bundles".

Self-approval and self-acceptance in the now are the main keys to positive changes in every area of our lives.

LOUISE HAY

Here is an example of wording you might use while tapping in doing The Setup. The Setup is followed by The Sequence / Reminder phrases:

The Setup
Even though I have this pain in my left knee, I deeply and completely accept myself.

Even though I have this pain in my left knee, I deeply and completely accept, respect and love myself.
Even though I have this pain in my left knee, I deeply and completely accept and forgive myself anyway.

The Setup only takes moments to do. After repeating The Setup three times, the next step is called The Sequence or Reminders.

The Sequence / Reminders

These steps are usually done in an order that begins at the top of the head, moving down the body in the specific sequence presented here. While tapping on the acupoints, simply repeat a word or phrase that is a reminder of the actual problem for which you are using EFT.

For example, if you repeated, three times during The Setup, *"Even though I have a fear of dogs, I deeply and completely love and accept myself"*, during the Sequence you could say, *"this fear of dogs....fear of dogs....my fear of dogs, ..."* while tapping on all of the tapping points.

> The idea is to use the wording of The Sequence as "reminders" of the problem that you are tapping to resolve.

> These reminders are best said out loud when possible because it is too easy for our thoughts to drift into other thoughts instead of staying focused on the one particular thing for which you are seeking to find relief with EFT.

As you read the description of the location of the tapping points, please refer to the illustrations. Note that tapping points, including those on the face, are on solid bone; they are not on any soft places such as the temples at the sides of the head.

Your notes about tapping points:

The Crown Point (CR)

The Crown Point is slightly in back of the center of the head. The Crown Point is not on the exact center of the head known as "the soft spot".

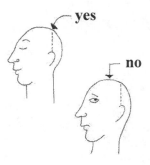

You can find this point by making an imaginary line from the top of both ears to the top of the head.

The Below the Nipple / Liver Points (BN)

These tapping points are easy to find in men; they are two centimeters (one inch) below the nipples. We often skip these points in working with women clients because the proximity to the breasts can make it awkward to tap on this area.

If I feel the need to tap on the liver points of female clients, which could be connected to a client's anger, I ask female clients to tap on that area themselves.

The 9-Gamut Procedure

In his instructional DVDs, Gary Craig uses the 9-Gamut if he is not making the typically fast progress of EFT. There are some EFT experts who prefer to always use the 9-Gamut. I do not always use it but I have seen notable benefits when I do add the 9-Gamut in situations where progress is slow or absent. The choice is yours. I suggest to my students that they try tapping both ways, with and without the 9-Gamut.

The 9-Gamut Tapping Spot

As mentioned above, the 9-Gamut Procedure is not always used. Here is a little history: In the early days of EFT in the 1990's, the 9-Gamut was always used. Gary Craig discovered, however, that excellent results could often be had with EFT, even without the 9-Gamut.

It is called the 9-Gamut simply because there are 9 steps. The entire procedure takes only about ten seconds. It is an odd-looking procedure with a good purpose. Its goal is to stimulate and balance both sides of the brain. It does so while tapping on a specific point of one hand, at the same time that the client is doing specific eye movements and either humming a known song or counting numbers.

Humming a song is a creative job of the right side of the brain while counting numbers engages the logical left side of the brain. You can easily do this procedure with clients and with yourself. With the exception of humming a song and counting, you or your client should stay focused on the problem by repeating the reminder word or phrase or continuing to tell your story.

The first few times you do the Gamut might feel awkward because you are doing several new things at the same time, but after a little practice, it will be completely natural to you. Tap on the Gamut point continuously while you are focused on the problem by repeating the reminder word or phrase. At the same time do the following actions. Here is an example for knee pain. Each action takes about a second or two:

1. Close both eyes.

This pain in my left knee.
2. Open both eyes with your head straight and look straight ahead.

This pain in my left knee.
3. Keep your head straight but point your eyes down towards the floor, looking to the right.

All this pain in my left knee.
4. Keep your head straight but point your eyes down towards the floor, looking to the left.

My left knee hurts.
5. Make a big circle with your eyes in one direction.

This pain in my left knee.
6. Change direction and make a big circle with your eyes to the left.

This pain in my left knee.

7. Hum two seconds of any song (for example: "The Happy Birthday Song" or "Twinkle, Twinkle Little Star" or any other song.)

8. Quickly count out loud numbers 1,2,3,4,5.

9. Hum two seconds of the same song from number 7 above. *Oh, what a beautiful day...*

<hr/>

Some Advanced Tapping Points

I usually add some or all of the advanced points to The Sequence if the basic points do not produce results. You can add some or any of the advanced points:

- at the end of the basic Sequence
- or you can add them at any time during the Sequence
- you can add them when your intuition tells you to add them

They are referred to in these pages as "advanced tapping points" or "advanced points" because they were incorporated into EFT after *The EFT Manual* was written. The following points do not replace the basic tapping points. They can be used as additional tapping points if progress is slow to arrive.

The Wrist Points

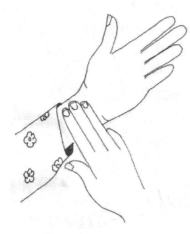

The Wrist Points are located on the inside of each wrist.

There are acupoints in this area that are primarily connected with stress, anxiety and sadness.

In addition to adding any or all of the following tapping points to the Sequence you can try, with clients where there is no visible progress from EFT, to ask them to repeat the words of the Setup with more feeling or animation. Depending on if you have neighbors or not, you can try asking your client to yell the words of the Setup. This often results in progress.

Each wrist point is easily found by putting the side of the ring finger (the side that is closest to the baby finger) of the hand that does the tapping along the crease of the wrist of the opposite hand. The ring, middle and index fingers of the tapping hand lightly slap on each wrist point about 7 to 9 times, more if preferred.

The Back of the Neck & Spine Points

Under your or your client's skull, above the back of the neck, you will find two small indentations. It is in those indentations that you gently make small circles with your thumbs; these indentations are not tapped.

As in the normal EFT Sequence, simply repeat the reminder phrase as you rub on these crevices, in small circles with your thumbs. The direction of the circles does not matter.

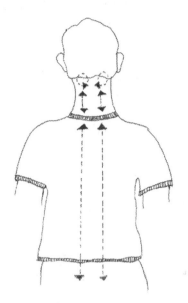

Similar to the Crown Point located at the top of the head, many energy meridians originate from the spine, wrapping around the chest and extending to meridians in various parts of the body. When tapping this area, do not tap on the spine itself. Use the four fingers of each hand to gently tap or rub along both sides of the spine, about two centimeters (one inch) on either side of the spinal column.

Start at the neck, below the skull and simply tap gently all along the length of the spine, ending at the lower back just before you reach the buttocks.

The Knee & Ankle Points

The Knees (K)

The knees are lightly slapped on the sides of the leg, just a little below the kneecaps while repeating the reminder phrase. Use the palms of both hands to lightly slap the inside and outside of each knee at the same time, one knee at a time. I have noticed particularly excellent results adding the knee points to The Sequence when clients, especially female clients, have low energy or are sad.

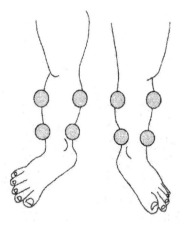

The Ankles (AN)

An important warning: the ankle points are never to be used on pregnant women. According to Traditional Chinese Medicine, this acupoint can be helpful in stimulating uterine contraction during the time that a woman gives birth. Obviously, one does not want uterine contraction before the time of delivery.

To find the correct location of the ankle tapping points, place your baby fingers of both hands slightly above the anklebone.

Then gently slap on both the inner and outer side of your leg while repeating the Reminder phrase.

The above pages do not include the detailed information about EFT that is easily available in many resources, in order to tap correctly. In addition to my books mentioned at the beginning of this chapter: *EFT & Life* e-Book (in English) and the published book, *EFT & Vita* (in Italian), there are many excellent ways to learn EFT. You will find a listing of some of them in The Resource Section.

...I don't mind saying that after talking to a thousand people who have had these (life after life) *experiences...it has given me great confidence that there is life after death.*

RAYMOND MOODY, MD, PhD

Chapter 10

THE FUTURE

We already know, through standard this lifetime EFT that amazing healings can occur simply by being in contact with the Energy System and, at the same time, focusing on the problem we want to resolve or clear. The documented medical and scientific research that validates this conclusion can be easily found in many places.

In listening to Esther Hicks, of Abraham-Hicks, talk about how we create our reality, she teaches: *when we ask it is given*. According to this teaching, we either receive or do not receive what we ask for depending on the level of our own resistance to receiving. Period! This "receiving" can happen in this lifetime as well as in our future lives. I recommend the teachings of Abraham-Hicks for the wisdom they contain.

There is a fascinating YouTube video, in particular, that I recommend because it refers to our future lives. In this brief 6 minute and 23 second video, you will also hear about the energetic drive behind the evolution of species! You might find yourself having one of those personal *"aha moments"* of understanding as I did while listening to this. If you have a computer, you can find it at www.youtube.com, "Asking Without Words".

Is Knowledge of Past Lives the Missing Ingredient to Health and Happiness?

What if the missing ingredient to human health and happiness, as well as the prevention of the illnesses that plague humanity, rests in the knowledge that life is eternal, that we have lived before and that we will live again?

What if, even in the middle of a crowded street, you begin to feel badly but you have learned to recognize that perhaps the new bad feeling is connected with a known or unknown memory from this or another lifetime? And what if you, after slipping out of the present moment, have learned how to regain the present, letting go of any negative re-stimulation that caused the sudden bad feeling to arrive in the first place?

Chances are that your total "return" to putting your attention in the present moment will be a key factor for your health and happiness.

> *The past is over and done and cannot be changed; the point of power is always in the present moment.*
>
> LOUISE L. HAY

There is, thanks mostly to the discoveries of quantum physics, a lot of interesting work being done in the area of future lives. What if we could really create our future lifetimes, without bringing with us the negative baggage we have accumulated from our past and distant past? Maybe our future lives are simply the other side of the same coin as our past lives and this future continues into forever?

Once my clients have cleared their present or past life issue or issues, I take great pleasure in introducing them to a tapping process that I call *A Future Window*. In this process, we simply bring into the session one or more positive attributes of what is often referred to as our "authentic self"—that which we feel is us at our very best.

A Future Window is a simple process of tapping on the acupoints, relaxing, feeling oneself in the now moment and, from the present, simply reviewing one's life and stopping at a memory that exemplifies what that person feels is his or her authentic best.

A male client contacted an event of helping a friend. I guided him, while tapping, to really feeling that feeling of helping the friend. Revisiting it. Reliving it. Really *being* who he feels is his authentic self by helping that friend.

Then, while continuing to tap, I asked him to imagine a time in the future of his own invention, in another body of his choice, maybe another century, maybe another country, wherever and whenever he chose, while he felt all that he felt while he was helping the friend in this lifetime.

The future event of helping a friend, while tapping on the points of the Energy System, can go into many aspects of future time. We can even imagine a future that includes people who have been "traveling" with us in various lifetimes being with us again and again. We would not want, however, to imagine our "ex" as a chicken in our future! ☺

Many people, who work professionally in the area of past and future lives, believe that we choose our parents. I also believe this to be true. Perhaps we make this choice to resolve a problem, to continue a vendetta against them or for a wide range of negative reasons.

My intention, however, with *A Future Window* is that maybe we can choose our new parents in a new future life because we like them or respect them or love them. Maybe we can choose the geographical area we want to live in, not because of our subconscious energetic fears but because we like the place.

Maybe we can be free from the weight of carrying negative past experiences with us as we move into future lifetimes. And maybe we can be the "us" that is happy and joyful and healthy, lifetime after lifetime. If we have lived before, it makes sense that our eternal energy selves will live again so we might as well do the best we can in this lifetime to ensure that our future lives are good in every way.

If we believe that we will be returning to live again, perhaps we can begin to plan our futures on this planet with the knowledge that all of us – family, friends, children, grandchildren, strangers, you and me – might all be returning to live on Earth. It is a benefit to all that we take darn good care of this planet.

Even though we are now approaching the final pages of this book, I still cannot say to you with total proof and scientific certainty that we have lived before or will live again in the future when we have finished with the body that we now have.

But I do know that by helping people and ourselves reach into the distant past of 500 or 5,000 years ago, we can use pretty much the same EFT techniques in pretty much the same way that we would help someone clear a trauma from 5 years or 5 minutes ago.

We are living with the same energy!

And so, in doing this work, for our clients, our patients, our families, friends and ourselves, the present and the future, can be safe places to be while we live our lives manifesting our healthy, happy, powerful and beautiful selves. Become free from all negative baggage? Feel the great joy of healing our past lives and living fully in the present moment? Be able to make this and future lifetimes fabulous? Become the full, whole, connected beings that we can be without looking outside ourselves to be happy? Become our genuine selves without the negative past *stuff* that we carry with us from negative past experiences that prevent us from becoming who we really are? Yes, all that, I do know with total certainty, is our true energetic potential.

A little while, a moment of rest upon the wind,
and another woman shall bear me.

KAHLIL GIBRAN

The Resource Section

➤ **Books about EFT**

Gary Craig has written many EFT books; here is a partial list:

The EFT Manual (includes *"The Personal Peace Procedure"*)

EFT for Back Pain

EFT for Weight Loss

EFT for PTSD (Post Traumatic Stress Disorder)

EFT for Sports Performance

Gary Craig, Donna Eden & David Feinstein, PhD:

The Healing Power of EFT and Energy Psychology;

The Promise of Energy Psychology

Gloria Arenson

EFT for Procrastination

Patricia Carrington, PhD

Discover the Power of Meridian Tapping

John Bullough & EFT Experts

EFT and Beyond

Jean Faithful

Better by Bedtime with EFT

Brad Yates
The Wizard's Wish
Fuel the Fire, Perform with Passion
The EFT Wizard's Big Book of Tapping Scripts

Karl Dawson and Sasha Allenby
Matrix Reimprinting Using EFT

Carol Look, PhD
Improve Your Eyesight with EFT
Attracting Abundance with EFT

Rue Hass
Opening the Cage of Pain with EFT
EFT for the Highly Sensitive Temperament
EFT for Fibromyalgia

Judith Rivera Rosso
*EFT & Life (*eBook)
*EFT & Vita (*in Italian, paperback)

Jack Canfield and Pamela Bruner
Tapping into Ultimate Success

Nick Ortner
The Tapping Solution

Sophia Cayer
EFT Language: Creating It and Going with the Flow (also
in Spanish)

Ron Ball and Joseph Mercola, DO
Freedom at Your Fingertips

Karin Davidson and Ann Adams
EFT Level 1-3 Comprehensive Training Resource
Course Books

Please note: Many of the other geniuses in the EFT community have written books; you can find them on the Internet, in bookstores and by checking their web sites.

➢ Books about past lives

Brian Weiss, MD:

Many Lives, Many Masters

Through Time into Healing

Same Soul, Many Bodies

Only Love is Real

*Meditation: Achieving Inner Peace and Tranquility in Your
    Life*

*Miracles Happen: The Transformational Healing Power of
    Past Life Memories* with Amy Weiss

Jim B. Tucker, MD

Life Before Life: Children's Memories of Previous Lives

Ian Stevenson, MD

Children Who Remember Previous Lives

Where Reincarnation and Biology Intersect

Raymond Moody, MD, PhD

Life After Life

Life After Loss

Glimpses of Eternity

Sandra Anne Taylor

The Hidden Power of Your Past Lives

Barbara Stone, PhD

*Invisible Roots: How Healing Past Life Trauma Can
    Liberate Your Present*

Andy Tomlinson

Healing the Eternal Soul

Exploring the Eternal Soul

Transforming the Eternal Soul

Michael Newton

Journey of Souls

Robert Schwartz

Your Soul's Plan

In addition, there are many other books on the subject that can easily be found in you bookstore and on the Internet.

➤ More great books

Dr. Roger Callahan (TFT)
Tapping the Healer Within
The Five-Minute Cure for Public Speaking and Other Fears

Donna Eden
Energy Medicine
Energy Medicine for Women

Jon Kabat-Zinn, PhD
Mindfulness for Beginners: Reclaiming the Present Moment and Your Life
Wherever You Go, There You Are
Letting Everything Become Your Teacher: 100 Lessons in Mindfulness

Shamash Alidina
Mindfulness for Dummies

Serafino Amoroso
Muscle Testing, Complete Nonsense or the Basis for Real Health Care?

Hans Selye, MD, PhD
The Stress of Life

Barbara Stone, PhD
Transforming Fear into Gold

Dawson Church, PhD
Genie in your Genes

Norman Cousins
Anatomy of an Illness, as Perceived by the Patient

Bruce Lipton, PhD
The Biology of Belief
Spontaneous Evolution

Gregg Braden
The Language of the Divine Matrix

Wayne W. Dyer, PhD
Excuses Be Gone!

Louise L. Hay
You Can Heal Your Life

Louise Hay and Cheryl Richardson
You Can Create an Exceptional Life

Herbert Benson, MD
The Relaxation Response

Bernie Siegel, MD
Love, Medicine & Miracles
Peace, Love & Healing
A Book of Miracles
How to Live Between Office Visits
101 Exercises for the Soul

Rhonda Byrne
The Secret
The Power

Dr. Masaru Emoto
The Hidden Messages in Water

Barbara Ann Brennan
Hands of Light

Mina Semyon
The Distracted Centipede – a Yoga Experience
You Don't Need to Die of Disappointment (upcoming)

Kahlil Gibran
The Prophet

Jack Canfield
The Principles of Success

Marci Shimoff
Happy for No Reason

Lissa Rankin, MD
Mind Over Medicine

Anita Moorjani
Dying to Be Me

Judith Orloff, MD
Emotional Freedom
Dr. Judith Orloff's Guide to Intuitive Healing
Second Sight

Pam Grout
E-Squared

The teachings of Abraham books by Esther and Jerry Hicks:
The Law of Attraction
Ask and It is Given
Money and the Law of Attraction
*The Vortex (*Plus all of their other books)

➤ EFT Internet sites

- www.eftitalia.com
  This is my EFT site in both English and Italian.

- www.emofree.com
  This is the "mother" of all EFT sites; it is hosted by the founder of EFT, Gary Craig. The site includes many free videos and the opportunity to purchase the vast library of Gray Craig's instructional videos.

- www.eftuniverse.com
  This site is a rich library of valuable information about EFT. It includes articles written by EFT practitioners, from medical professionals to loving parents and grandparents. The web site also includes the results of

independent scientific research done to test and explain the phenomenal successes of EFT.

From this site, you can download and print, free of cost, a mini version of the original EFT Manual written by Gary Craig and the full version as a free download translated into 22 languages. The site also contains films showing actual demonstrations of EFT in action.

Most of the site has been translated into Spanish and will soon be available in French. You can also use this site to locate EFT teachers and Certified EFT Practitioners throughout the world. On this extensive site, you will also find free videos that demonstrate important details on the correct application of EFT.

- www.eftmastersworldwide.com
Many years ago, Gary Craig taught classes of EFT to a group of 29 professional practitioners from eight countries. He later gave the title of "EFT Master" to those who completed those classes. Each of the EFT Masters is highly respected in the EFT community and recognized as being extremely skilled in delivering EFT.

Over the years, EFT has grown and expanded so that the original training received by the group of EFT Masters has become available throughout various classes taught by EFT teachers, including myself. You can find all of the original EFT Masters along with their personal web sites and contact information, books and articles on this site.

- www.rogercallahan.com
  The late Dr. Roger Callahan was a psychologist and one of the early pioneers to tap on the energy meridians. He created Thought Field Therapy (TFT) similar. His wife, Joanne, is continuing Dr. Callahan's work. TFT has been adopted by Sir Richard Branson's Virgin Airlines to help passengers use tapping to overcome their fear of flying. The actress Whoppie Goldberg, who overcame this fear, has become an active and entertaining spokeswoman for tapping.

  > *I once heard Gary Craig on a video refer to EFT practitioners as a caring and generous group of people. In my experience, I have found the EFT community of professional "tappers" to be readily available to share their knowledge and valuable experience. It is not possible to list all of them here; out of the many excellent, experienced and caring tappers in the world, here are a few:*

- www.eft-tap.com
  Pro EFT™ Master Dr. Kiya Immergluck, a psychotherapist, has contributed examples of her excellent work to my previous books. She has earned the Pro Master title through a training program created by EFT Master Lindsay Kenny.

- www.LKCoaching.com
  EFT Master Lindsay Kenny is well known for her many innovative EFT techniques: Bundling Baggage, The

Tapping Tree, The Golden Gate Technique, The Pro EFT™ Master Program, The Ultimate Truth Statement, The Tower of Shame Technique just to name a few of her outstanding contributions.

- www.tapintoheaven.com
  This is the site of Gwenn Bonnell, an expert in using EFT and well known for her work in teaching how to help animals using Surrogate EFT.

- www.bradyates.net
  You can see about 70 EFT videos on YouTube of Brad Yates as well as Brad and children using EFT.

  Brad was formerly a famous clown in the Barnum & Bailey Circus and enjoys bringing some of his clown experience into his work with EFT. You might find him tapping on YouTube while wearing his big red clown nose. ☺

- www.ingridinter.com
  In addition to helping people in many areas with EFT, Ingrid Dinter is also specialized in issues of anger and betrayal.

- www.beacontraining.co.uk
  EFT Master Jacqui Crooks also offers life-enhancing EFT training in the United Kingdom.

- www.sophiacayer.com

EFT Master Sophia Cayer specializes in helping people with issues of trauma and abuse.

- www.emofree.it
  Andrew Lewis, an Australian EFT practitioner and trainer, works in both English and Italian. He specializes in teaching EFT as a tool for self-empowerment and self-healing.

- www.deepliving com
  Bennie Naudé's work as an EFT practitioner includes teaching EFT to students around the world.

- www.allergyantidotes.com
  Sandi Radomski, is brilliant in using EFT to help children and adults overcome their allergies and food intolerances.

- www.how to tap.com
  Karin Davidson gives a lot of EFT information on her site. She also presents clear information about a fairly new and important advanced EFT technique called Matrix Re-imprinting, originally developed by Karl Dawson and Sasha Allenby, in which she is an expert.

  I have also been having excellent results for my clients and myself using the methods of Matrix Re-imprinting and I highly support its innovations. JRR

- www.efthub.com

Here you can find a vast library of audio and video interviews with many EFT experts discussing their approaches to using EFT to resolve a wide range of problems.

- www.thrivingnow.com
  A resource for learning and sharing for the EFT community.

- www.mercola.com
  This major web site, under the direction of noted EFT expert, Dr. Joseph Mercola, is the most visited alternative medicine site on the entire Internet.

  Dr. Mercola, himself an EFT tapper, is also a published EFT author. On Dr. Mercola's website you can follow along with several tapping demonstrations by the EFT expert, Julie Schiffman.

- www.masteringeft.com
  This is the web site of Patricia Carrington, PhD. Dr. Carrington is an EFT Master, Associate Clinical Professor at The Robert Wood Johnson Medical School, former faculty member in the Department of Psychology at Princeton University and has won awards for her work in mental health. She is also the author of a long list of professional publications. Dr. Carrington is celebrated throughout the world for her work in EFT and as the originator of *The EFT Choices Method*.

- www.attractingabundance.com

This is the site of Carol Look, PhD. Dr. Look has a distinguished background in traditional psychotherapy with a Doctoral Degree in Clinical Hypnotherapy. Since discovering EFT, she has personally helped thousands of people throughout the world.

- www.cascinarosso.info
  My husband Adriano Rosso and I have restored a lovely group of very old stone buildings on a gorgeous hillside in northern Italy. This is our home base for teaching and giving private sessions.

Guests arrive here from many parts of the world with the option of benefiting from EFT and/or Usui Reiki or Karuna Reiki® while they stay in cozy apartments and enjoy the breathtaking natural surroundings of our farm. Our guests also enjoy the delicious organic vegetables, fruit and berries grown here at Cascina Rosso ☺.

> ## ➤ EFT Radio & Audio Sites

- www.eft-talk.com
  Rick Wilkes has teamed up with Dr. Carol Look to create audio information via the Internet on how to use the various approaches and techniques of EFT.

- www.blogtalkradioonline.com
  Eleanore Duyndam of New Zealand interviews EFT experts on a wide variety of practical subjects.

> ## ➤ EFT Films

- *Introduction to EFT*

This is a 7-minute video in English on the web site www.eftuniverse.com.

- *Operation Emotional Freedom: The Answer*
  A powerful documentary created by Gary Craig and a group of EFT experts. The film focuses on the fact that one out of every three combat veterans who return from any war comes home with PTSD (Post Traumatic Stress Disorder). EFT is clearly shown to be an important answer to the serious question of how they can be free from their suffering.

- *The Tapping Solution* (formerly *Try it on Everything*)
  Created by the dynamic brother and sister team Nick and Jessica Ortner, this documentary film follows the experiences of a group of people who, unfamiliar with EFT at first, learn about EFT and receive tapping for their individual problems such as pain, fear, overweight, serious illness, etc.

  The Ortner's are also the creators of "The Tapping World Summit", a ten day, free annual event on the Internet where EFT experts from around the world share their approaches to using EFT. "The Tapping Solution" DVD contains a tapping demonstration by Nick Ortner.

Note: EFT Tapping Demonstration Videos
There are many demonstrations of EFT tapping on the Internet; not all of the videos on the Internet show you correct tapping. Some of the above sites include tapping videos; all of them demonstrate EFT correctly. You

can simply follow along with the demonstrations and substitute your particular problem if it is different from the example used for the demonstration.

I believe that when the body dies,
consciousness continues to exist
and relocates or reincarnates
into a new body in a circle of life.

BERNIE SIEGEL, MD

Epilogue

Sometimes my EFT students feel frustrated after they have personally experienced the benefits of EFT. Their frustration happens when they go out into the world to share their knowledge but meet people who refuse to try EFT to resolve problems of this or a past lifetime. As the true old saying goes, "It takes all kinds of people to make a world!" Another old saying "You can lead a horse to water but you can't make him drink it!" is also true.

This beautiful world of ours is filled with many people who have been conditioned to stubbornly refuse natural healing methods. When you meet them, I suggest that after you do your best to explain the potential benefits that can await them with EFT, but if they refuse your help, realize that we cannot change people. People can only change themselves if that's what they want to do.

I am personally not anti-medicine nor against medical care. There are, however, widespread habits of dependency on pharmaceutical drugs just as there are on toxic chemicals used in our soil, plant life, drinking water and the air we breathe.

There is also a huge amount of easily available information and education about the vital life-giving benefits of a more natural way of life. Some, unfortunately, will reject or not hear those messages. As I tell my students, you can be happy with the idea that maybe those who refuse your help today will "hear" the message in a future lifetime. ☺

It has become a new personal tradition of mine to include, in my EFT books, a poem that I wrote to the Founder of EFT; it is a little "thank you" for this amazing healing gift to the world of EFT.

An Ode to Gary Craig

In this world where pain and sorrow
Could enter every door
There came a man
Named Gary Craig
Who said,
"No more! No more!"
"You can be free!"
He told us all
Just learn some simple steps
Then do it, teach it and spread the word
Take it to its awesome depths.
He gave it the name of EFT
A precious gift for all and me
And said to us,
"Here is your liberty!
"You can be healthy, happy and free!"
His gift has reached even me
On a mountaintop in Italy.
The whole world is, in fact,
An even better place
Because Gary Craig has taught us
How to tap upon our face.

In working with EFT clients and their past lives, the trauma of war sometimes comes up. I wrote this little poem after concluding one of those sessions.

Remembering Peace

Today you attack me
Tomorrow I attack you
Attacking hurts me
It hurts you.
Let us put down our war tools
These ugly toys
And instead
Let us laugh together
Let us share memories
Hug
Respect
Honor each other and ourselves.
If that doesn't work
We can always attack each other again
And again
Until the end of time.

*When we resolve trauma
from any one of our lives,
that improvement affects all of our lives
simultaneously,
including the present one.*

BARBARA STONE, PHD

About the Author

Judith Rivera Rosso was born and raised in North America where her earliest dreams were to become a doctor. Instead, an illness in college caused her to abandon medicine. She became a professional sculptor and teacher, writing and producing television and radio documentaries as well as independent films. Her work for Public Television and Radio included *American Women in Prison, Crime & the Senior Citizen, The Haitian Refugees, The Vietnamese Refugees, The Truth about Emergency Medical Care, Actualities: The Prison Story* (Public Radio) and many others. The Holocaust film, *In Their Words*, was honored with a "Best Film of the Year" award by the National Council of Christians and Jews.

She currently lives and works in northern Italy with her husband Adriano Rosso. Together, they have restored a group of old Italian farmhouses where they have created The Cascina Rosso Organic Farm and Bed & Breakfast. Guests come to Cascina Rosso from many parts of the world to spend their vacations in the breathtaking natural paradise of hills and valleys. Guests can also choose to study EFT with Judy or have private EFT sessions. Judy and Adriano are both Reiki Masters so guests to The Cascina are also able to study both Usui and Karuna Reiki®

with Adriano. Judy and Adriano are the sole representatives in Italy for Karuna Reiki®. Judy is an EFT teacher-trainer and Certified EFT practitioner. In addition to *The Great Joy of Healing Past Lives*, she has written the book *EFT & Vita* in Italian and the English language e-Book, *EFT & Life* as well as numerous articles on specific applications of EFT.

To inquire about Judy's classes or private sessions, you can contact her office at: The Cascina Rosso Organic Farm / *Agriturismo Biologico Cascina Rosso*
Web Sites: www.eftitalia.com; www.cascinarosso.info
Email: eft-italy@libero.it; rosso.cascina@libero.it
Tel: (+39) 0144-93100

Index

A

abilities 1, 7, 17, 23, 29
Abraham 104, 114
acupoints 17, 42, 49, 55, 56, 71, 73,
    75, 77, 99, 102,106
addictions 3
Advanced Tapping Points 99
Agriturismo, Cascina Rosso 76
allergies 2
anger 3
ankles 102
anxiety 2, 46
Applied Kinesiology 29
Art of EFT, The 23
authentic self 106
Automatic Clients 22, 65

B

Back of the Neck & Spine 100
    (illustration), 101
Believer Clients 21, 43, 53
Benson, Herbert, MD 19
bio-tensor 32 (*photo*graph), 32-34,
    45-49, 54, 55, 59, 60, 68, 69,
    77, 79, 83

birth 44, 52, 102
Bonte-Friedheim, Luise xviii
Braden, Gregg xliii, 113
breathing 52, 62, 68
Brennan, Barbara, PhD xliii

C

Callahan, Roger, PhD xli, 1,112
Canfield, Hansen, Hawthorne &
    Shimoff 19
Canfield, Jack v, xliii, 52, 110, 113
Cascina Rosso 76, 127, 129
cells 16
child 23, 39, 48, 54, 55, 70, 72, 75
Child Clients 23, 72
childhood 44
children xxiii, 23, 72, 73, 107, 111
Chopra, Deepak, MD v, 27, 78
Clue-Giver Clients 23, 70
clues 23, 70
cognitive shift 79
confidential 46
conscious 6, 23-26, 32
consciously 16, 24, 25, 52, 53,
    64, 79
consciousness 15, 78

continuous 78

core 15, 47

Craig, Gary xli, xliii, xliv, 1- 3,
    23-25, 34, 37, 46, 77, 109,
    114, 124

creativity 29

Crooks, Jaqui xi

Crown Points 96 (*illustration*)

D

Davidson, Karin xiv

death 57, 70, 78, 103

dehydrated 59

depression 2

Dewar, Thomas xliv

diseases 2

distant past 25, 42, 49-51, 106, 108

dowsing 31, 32

dowsing rod 30

Dyer, Wayne, PhD xliii, 16

E

eating disorders / problems 2, 76

Eden, Donna v, xliii, 109, 112

EFT v, xxxvii, 1-3, 5, 6, 16, 18,
    22-25, 28, 29, 33, 34, 36-38,
    40-42, 44-46, 49, 50, 52-60,
    64-66, 68-74, 77, 79, 99,
    100, 103, 104, 108- 110, 114

EFT & Life 86, 134

EFT & Vita 86, 103, 134

EFT Manual, The 88, 89, 99

Einstein, Albert, PhD 26, 30

Emerson, Ralph Waldo 17

emotional xxxvii, 1, 2, 24, 37, 41,
    50, 68, 71, 77

Emotional Freedom Techniques
    xxxvii

energetic potential 108

energetic response 26, 29, 30

Energy 2, 15-18, 24, 29, 31, 32, 41,
    44, 77, 79, 101, 102, 104,
    107- 109,112

energy field 16

Energy System 2, 14, 16, 18,
    24, 41, 77, 79, 86- 88, 92,
    104, 107

eternal xxiii, 5, 18, 28, 105, 107

event 22, 23, 25, 26, 40, 41, 46, 48-
    50, 54, 56, 57, 64-67, 72, 75,
    77, 78, 106, 107

evolution / evolving 18, 105

F

fear 2, 5, 25, 38, 40-42, 107

Feel As If Technique, The 42

Feinstein , David, PhD xliii, 109

fingertips 2, 61, 68

Ford, Henry xxxix

freeze response 41

future 26, 104, 106-108

Future Window, A 106, 107

G

Gallup Poll 4

Gandhi, Mahatma 85

Gerber, Markus xlii

Ghibaudi, Antonella xx

Gibran, Kahlil 108

glaucoma xlii, 53

Goodheart, George, DC 29

Grazi-Knapp, Irmela, MD xiv

H

Harris Poll 4
Harrison, George 65
Hay, Louise v, xliii, 105, 113
headaches 58-61
healing xxiii, xxxvii, xxxviii, 2,
        4, 6, 7, 17, 28-30, 56, 76-78,
        109, 111
hearing problems 67
Heart Math Institute, The 9
Hicks, Esther xliii, 104
Hicks, Esther & Jerry 13, 114
humor 69
hypnosis 6, 56

I

imagination xxxvii, 5, 41, 47, 73
imagine 6, 15, 39, 40, 51, 61, 62,
        68, 74, 106, 107
Immergluck, Kiya, PhD xii, xli
immortal xxiii, 17, 23
impressions 46
infancy 44
insomnia 2
instruments, energetic 16, 26, 30,
        34, 46, 54
intention 41, 45, 60, 68, 107
intuition 26, 27, 30, 32, 40, 99

J

Jung, Carl, MD 21

K

Kabat-Zinn, Jon, PhD 27

Karate Chop Point 60, 91, 92
        (*illustration*)
Keller, Helen 19
Kenny , Lindsay viii
kinesiology 54, 59, 60
Knee & Ankle Points 102
        (*illustration*)
Krassner, Paul 109

L

Law of Attraction, The 13
Lewis, Andrew xvii
Lewis, Pam xlii
lifetimes xxxvii, 2, 17, 36, 49, 77-
        79, 106, 107
limiting beliefs 6, 79
Lin, Chien-Hao 7
Lindstrom, Wade xvii, xlii
Lipton, Bruce, PhD v, xliii, 23,
        25, 112
London, Jack 67
love 17, 18, 69, 72, 107
low self-esteem 2

M

Mackay, Shekoofeh xx
Mackay, Yasmin xix
Matrix Reimprinting 50, 69, 110
meditation 27, 52
Mercola, Joe, DO v
meridian tapping 1
meridians 16, 77, 101
metaphors 22
method xxxvii, 1, 2, 26-30, 49, 56,
        59, 61, 62, 66
mind 6, 7, 26, 27, 39-41, 68, 103

mindful meditation 27

Moody, Raymond, MD, PhD
    103, 111

Moore-Hafter, Betty ix

muscle-testing 29, 30, 34, 47, 59,
    66, 76, 79

N

Naudé, Bennie x

negative 1, 6, 16, 17, 23, 24, 26, 29,
    30, 33, 40, 41, 45, 50, 51, 71,
    79, 105-108

Nietzsche, Freidrich 35

9-Gamut Procedure / Tapping
    Spot 96-99

O

objective 26, 27, 32

opinion 27, 41, 76

ourselves xxxvii, 6, 27, 62, 108

P

pain 2, 58-61, 66, 98, 99

Palmer, Lilli 19

past life incident 60

past life regression 56

Past Life Session Categories 21

Past Life Stress 8, 22

Past Life Trauma Sequence 8,
    10, 70

past lives xxiii, xxxvii, 2, 4- 7, 17,
    18, 22, 23, 29, 34, 37-39, 42-
    44, 56, 64, 68, 71, 72, 105,
    106, 111

Patton, General George S. 72

pendulum 31-34, 33 (*photograph*),
    46, 47, 54, 59, 60, 63, 66,
    73, 79

Personal Peace Procedure 34, 109

phobias 2

physical xxxvii, 1, 2, 5, 6, 16, 17,
    24, 29, 37, 43, 50, 58, 60, 64,
    65, 78, 79

physical shaking 40

PLS 8

PLTS 8, 10, 12, 14, 21, 70

positive statements 75

pre-conceived opinions 59

present moment 28, 52, 53, 64, 105

pretending 72-74

prevention 105

psychological 2, 6

psychological reversal 88

PTSD 2, 109

Q

quantum physics 105

questions 26, 29, 34, 37, 41, 47-49,
    54, 55, 57, 59-61, 68, 69,
    73, 76-79

R

radiesthesia 31

Randomski, Sandra, ND 92

rapport 37

Reid, Gary xlii

Reiki 120, 127

reincarnation xxxix, 5, 109

relaxation 61

relaxation response 10

relaxed 39, 46, 55, 60, 67

reminder phrases 40, 50, 61, 63, 94

research 32, 104, 115

resistance 37, 38, 42, 104

resistant clients 37, 38

resolution 38, 45, 47

responsibility 44, 63

revisit 7, 17

revisiting memories xxxvii

Rogers, Bel xxi

Rosso, Adriano xli, 120, 127

rounds 40, 50, 55, 61, 63, 71, 74, 78

rounds of tapping 78

S

sadness 3

Scarsi, Andrea xiii

Schopenhauer, Arthur, PhD 52

scientific xxxvii, 104, 108, 115

Selye, Hans, MD, PhD 8

Semyon, Mina xix, xlii

Sequence, The 99, 102

sessions 26, 34, 36, 39, 45, 47, 49,
    50, 54, 58, 59, 66, 70, 73, 79

Set-Up, The 50, 92-94

Siegel, Bernie, MD xxxi, 19,
    113, 122

sinus problem. 71

skeptical 42

Skeptical Clients 22, 47

Skype 65, 66, 70

sore spots 92

soul xxiii, 15-17

speaking softly and slowly 55

specific events 22, 26, 24, 43

spinal column 101

spirit xxiii, 15

Steiner, Rudolph, PhD 28

Stevenson, Ian, MD 75, 111

Stone, Barbara, PhD xi, 111, 125

stress 2, 9, 10, 17, 44

subconscious 6, 24-26, 32, 47, 50,
    51, 53, 55, 61, 62, 68, 69,
    71, 107

subconsciously 16, 79

SUD 66

surrogate 74-76

symbols 22

sympathetic problems 62

T

talents 1, 17, 23, 29

tapping 1, 2, 16, 22, 39, 40- 42, 44-
    47, 49, 54- 57, 61-64, 71-75,
    77, 78, 97, 99-101, 106, 107

tapping points 89, 90
    (*illustration*), 95

Taylor, Sandra Anne xxiii

Tearless Trauma 77

techniques 6, 24, 26, 54, 69, 108

TFT 1, 2, 112

Thomas, Bettina xviii

Thought Field Therapy 1

Tiller, William, PhD 32

Tolstoy, Leo 42

trauma 25, 36, 41, 58, 62, 64, 68,
    77, 79, 108

Tucker, Jim B., MD xxiii, 81, 111

U

understanding 51, 70, 105

unexplained upsets 51

V

vision problem 54
Vitale, Joe v
von der Weid, Diane xvi
von Goethe, Johann Wolfgang 58

W

warnings 52
weight 3, 73, 80, 107
Weiss, Brian, MD xxiii, 14, 27,
        56, 111
whispering 55
Whitman, Walt 70
womb 44
words of the client 57
Wrist Points 100 (*illustration*)

Y

Yates, Brad xiv
yellow alerts 52

Z

zzztts 24, 77

LEARN EFT TAPPING
WITH THE EFT E-BOOK

EFT & LIFE

by Judith Rivera Rosso

For information and to order your copy:
see: www.eftitalia.com
E-mail: eft-italy@libero.it

Also available as a
paperback book in Italian,
EFT & Vita

ISBN 978-88-905695-0-0
Published by:
Positivamente in Langa
Roccaverano, Italia